BEYOND WHERE WILTSHIRE MEETS SOMERSET

Cover: The bridge at Freshford across the River Frome, a short distance from its confluence with the Bristol Avon (Walk 9)

Overleaf: The delightful shallow valley west of Newton St Loe (Walk 13)

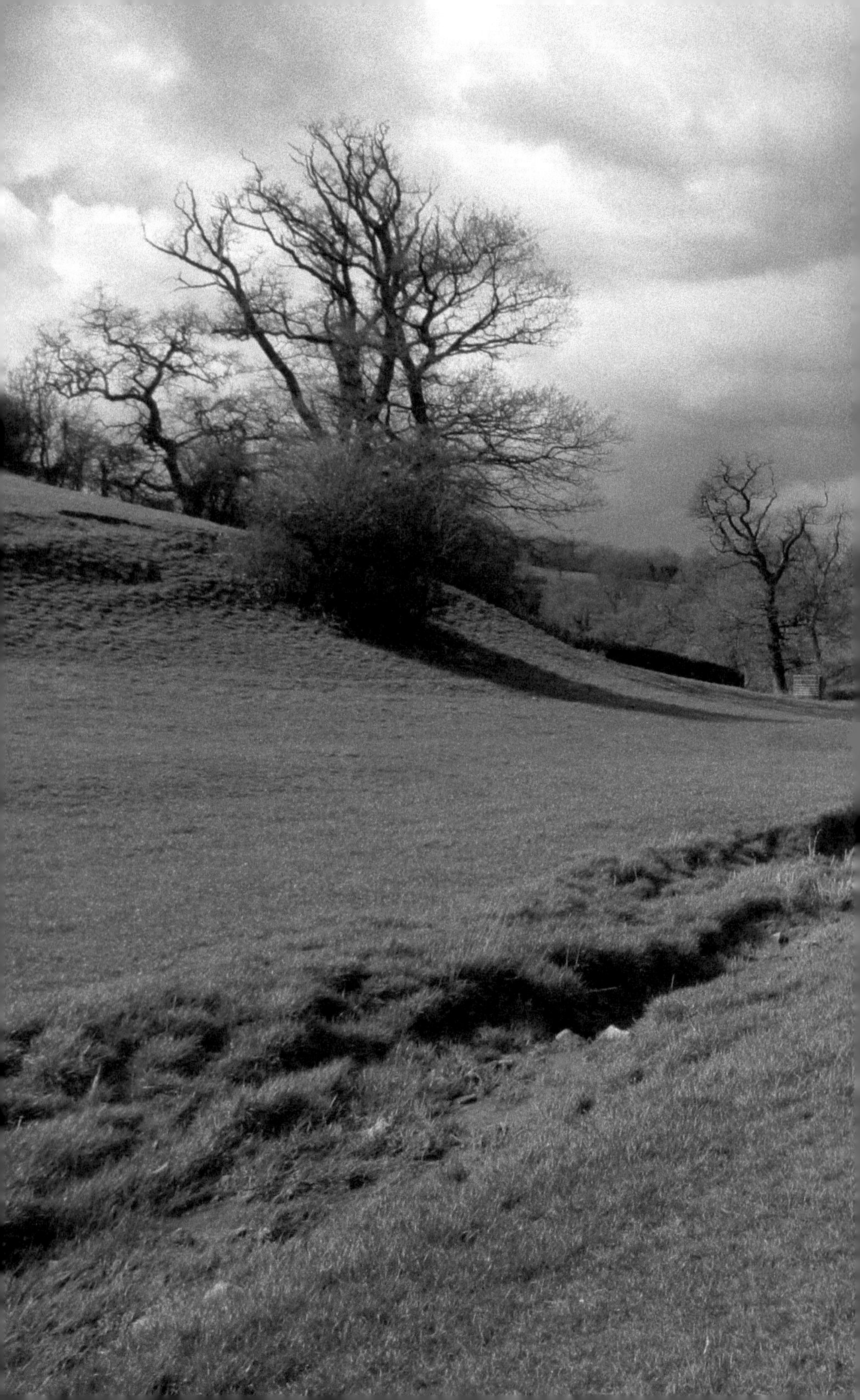

Beyond
Where Wiltshire
Meets Somerset

20 More Best Walks in the Country around Bath, Bradford on Avon, Trowbridge, Westbury, Warminster & Frome – plus Box and Corsham

Roger Jones

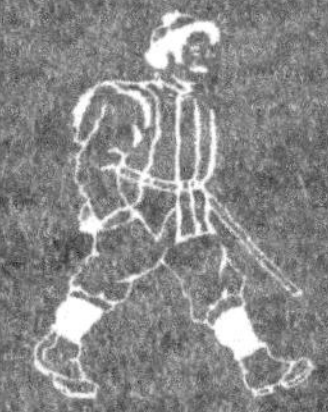

EX LIBRIS PRESS

First published 2015
Revised and updated editions
published in 2019 and 2023
EX LIBRIS PRESS
11 Regents Place
Bradford on Avon
Wiltshire   BA15 1ED

www.ex-librisbooks.co.uk

Origination by Ex Libris Press

Printed by CPI Anthony Rowe
Chippenham, Wiltshire

ISBN 978-1-906641-76-4

CONTENTS

Introduction

Where Wiltshire Meets Somerset, the book of local walks I published in 1982, has been continually in print. Walking all the routes again in the winter of 2012/13 in preparation for a revised edition, I enjoyed them so much that, during the following winter/spring, I was tempted to explore new routes within reasonably easy reach of home in Bradford on Avon. I have enjoyed this task enormously and succeeded in plotting 20 new walks in the area either side of the Wiltshire/Somerset border, once again in the environs of Bath, Bradford on Avon, Trowbridge, Westbury, Warminster and Frome but now going a little further to include Box and Corsham.

The front cover illustration of the present book depicts the focus of the walks in both books. It shows the River Frome where it is bridged at Freshford, just before it joins the Avon. The Frome has its source in the hinterland of Somerset to the south and west. Indeed the walks centred on the villages of Mells, Nunney and Wellow are all watered by streams which flow into the Frome. Similarly Batheaston, Bratton, Faulkland, Newton St Loe, Priston and Swainswick are drained by streams which eventually flow into the Avon. This Avon (the old British word for river) is generally referred to as the Bristol Avon, in order to distinguish it from other Avons. Two of the walks from villages featured in this book – Heytesbury and Sutton Veny – are situated beside the River Wylye, a tributary of the Salisbury Avon.

As the title of this second volume suggests, many, though not all of the walks are 'beyond' those described in the first book. One of my rules was that these new walks should avoid, wherever possible, contact with busy main roads; in revisiting the routes in the original book, I was reminded how unpleasant it can be to encounter them in the course of a ramble. Unfortunately, there are many such roads criss-crossing the hinterland between Bath and towns to the south-east, namely the A36 from Bath to Warminster and beyond, the A363 from Bathford via Bradford on Avon to Trowbridge; the A350 between Trowbridge via Westbury which joins the A36 at the Warminster bypass; and finally the A361 which links Trowbridge to the Frome bypass and continues to Nunney Catch and beyond. With one or two exceptions, all the walks here manage to avoid negotiating main roads, and then only for very short stretches or merely to cross over – but do take care!

The walks themselves demand a reasonable level of fitness. I was in my thirties when I researched *Where Wiltshire Meets Somerset*; I am now in my late 70s and must admit to getting a bit puffed on some of the steeper uphill sections – and sharp downhill stretches can be hard on the knees. Yet one of the joys of the countryside hereabouts are the frequent hills and valleys – it often seems that no sooner has one descended a slope than one must climb up again, but there is always the reward of changing perspectives and long views.

Thanks to the popularity of country walking and the efforts of local authorities and local branches of the Ramblers, rights of way and field crossings have never been as clearly marked and easy to negotiate as they are today. So long as one remains alert, it is not difficult to find one's way. We've experienced the COVID Pandemic since the previous edition of this book; the restrictions to which we were subject at that time encouraged many of us to explore our immediate locality.

Despite these advances, I do regret the loss of locally crafted stiles and gates – so many have been replaced by standard issue wooden or metal kissing gates. There is no doubt that they provide robust and easily negotiated crossings. It is always a pleasure to encounter an old stone slab or squeezer stile which makes use of the readily available local stone or timber. And sometimes a stile or gate has an unusual and quirky design, no doubt fashioned by the village mason, carpenter or blacksmith. Many such locally crafted stiles have been replaced with new metal gates which, it must be admitted, are smart and efficeint and, for many, more user-friendly. At the same time one cannot help regretting the disappearance of a locally crafted stile to an original design.

The walks in *Where Wiltshire Meets Somerset* were evenly split between the two counties. I have not quite managed an even distribution this time: ten are in Somerset; seven in Wiltshire and two straddle both counties whilst the walk from Swineford strays into South Gloucestershire.

Villages continue to evolve but remain an enduring and often attractive feature of the countryside. Amenities such as schools, shops, pubs, churches and chapels have sometimes been lost though there does now appear to be a reversal of this decline. Community-run shops and farm shops have opened in some fortunate villages, even community pubs. Whilst perhaps a minority of villages in this book are still served by a local shop, the majority retain their pub and church. Pub opening times are sometimes rather restricted and, disappointingly, churches are frequently found locked and bolted though it is always a pleasure to find one which is open and accessible.

Each of the 20 routes described here is accompanied by an appropriate sketch map to show the route taken and the main features to be seen. The maps, together with the detailed descriptions, I trust will be sufficient to guide the rambler. However, anyone with a serious interest is recommended to acquire the relevant Ordnance Survey maps. The two sets of maps listed below include the routes of all the walks in this book. The Explorer maps are twice the scale of the Landrangers and therefore offer more detail; in particular, all field boundaries are indicated so they are certainly more helpful for off-road walking.

Explorer Series 1:25,000

*(All public rights of way are
    in red)*
Sheet 155: Bristol and Bath

Sheet 156: Chippenham &

   Bradford-on-Avon

Sheet 142: Frome & Shepton Mallet

Sheet 143: Warminster & Trowbridge

Landranger Series 1: 50,000

*(All public rights of way are
    shown in green)*
Sheet 172: Bristol and Bath

Sheet 173: Swindon & Devizes

Sheet 183: Yeovil & Frome

Sheet 184: Salisbury & the Plain

The Walks

For convenience, and to save space in the section in each walk giving directions, I have adopted some abbreviations for oft-repeated words, as follows:

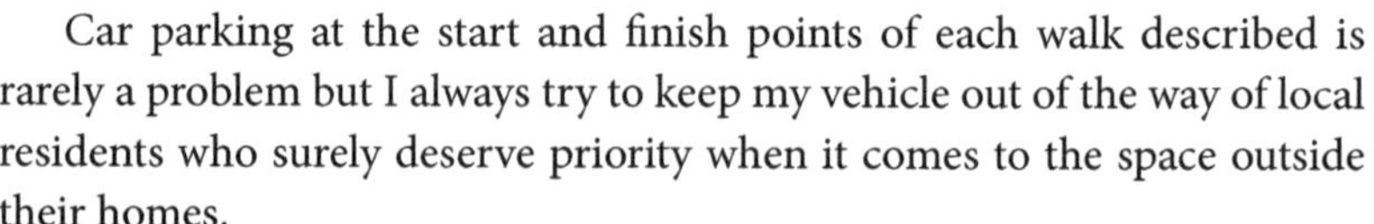

PF   Public Footpath, shown by a variety of signs

L   Left, as in turn L

R   Right

ST   Stile

XG   Kissing Gate

Key to the maps is as follows

Route along lane, road: ═══════════

Route along track ▬ ▬ ▬ ▬ ▬ ▬

Route along footpath ● ● ● ● ● ● ● ● ● ● ● ● ● ● ● ●

Railway track ┼┼┼┼┼┼┼┼┼┼┼┼┼┼┼┼┼┼┼┼┼┼┼┼

Car parking at the start and finish points of each walk described is rarely a problem but I always try to keep my vehicle out of the way of local residents who surely deserve priority when it comes to the space outside their homes.

Many of the villages and towns cited are served by some form of public transport though bus times can be very restricted, sometimes to a limited number of days per week. Bus services are under constant revision so do plan ahead if you intend using public transport.

I have noted local pubs under the heading 'Refreshments en route' in the introductory sections. However, many village pubs have restricted opening hours whilst others close in the cold winter season but open again when conditions improve. Some have closed altogether. Thus it is advisable to enquire first before planning an outing with a pub stop.

In previous books I have included 'Historical Notes' on places visited. This seems rather superfluous in these days of the world wide web when, at the click of a mouse, a wealth of information on people and places is immediately accessible. Thanks to Wikipedia and the like it is no longer necessary to quarry the pages of old topographical books to unearth morsels of information. The on-line Wiltshire Community History is a superb resource for many communities within the county.

I've enjoyed walking all the routes in the first weeks of 2023 in preparation for this new edition of *Beyond Where Wiltshire Meets Somerset*. and found them generally more easily accessible than previously. I've noted instances where minor changes have occurred on some of the routes, or where I could have been clearer in my route descriptions, and have done my best to amend the text accordingly.

The only real problem which may be encountered in July and August is a vigorous growth of maize, growing to a height well in excess of the likely walker, which completely blocks the way across fields. Nor may there be sufficient space at the field edge to allow an alternate passage. But sometimes, walkers (with the help of the farmer) have created a clear path through – see below.

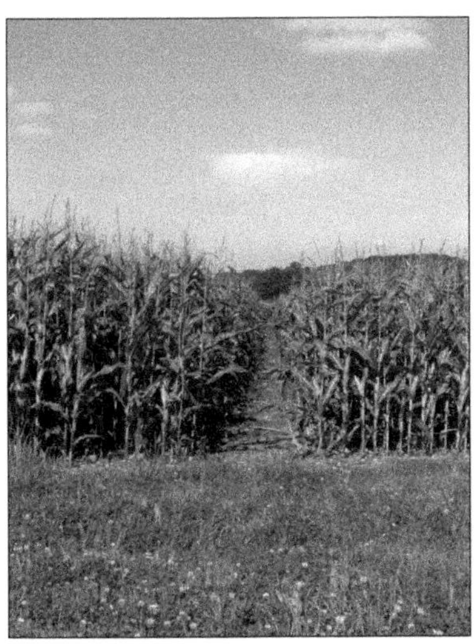
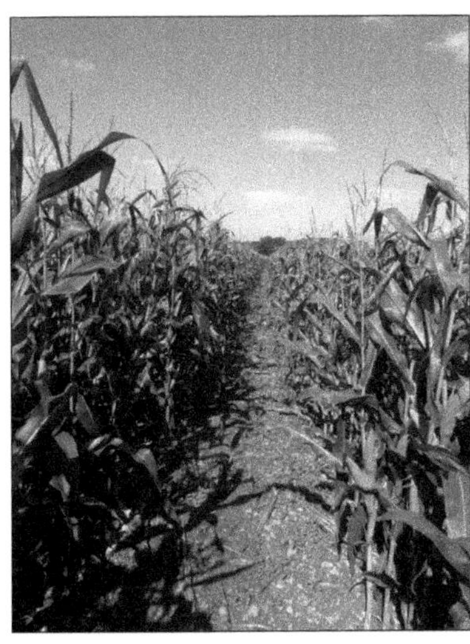

A welcome path through a field of maize. Unfortunately. not always typical.

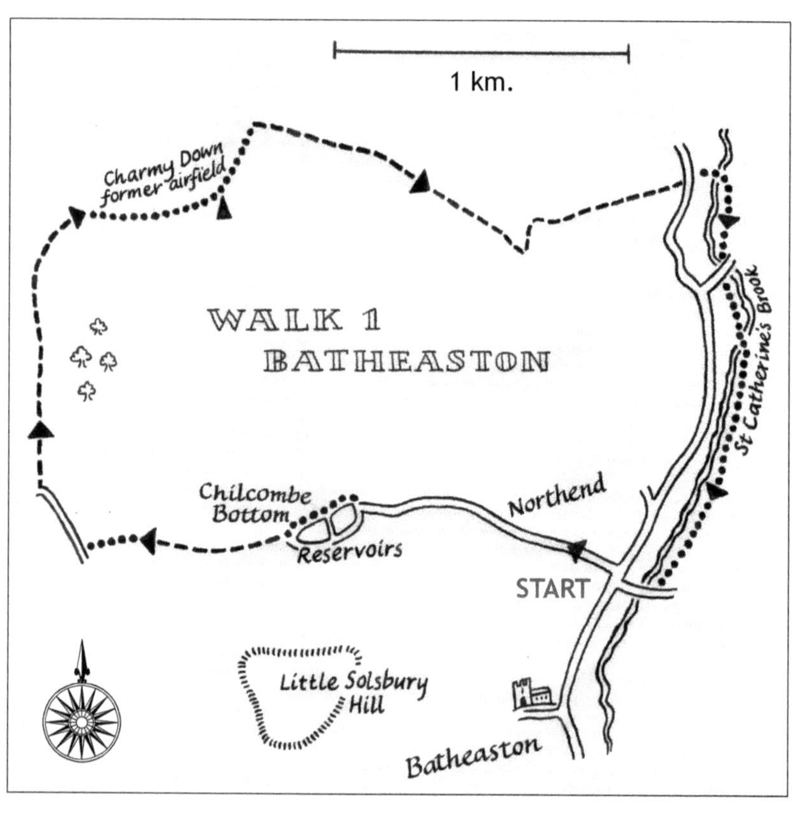

1 km.
Charmy Down
former airfield
WALK 1
BATHEASTON
St Catherine's Brook
Chilcombe
Bottom
Reservoirs
Northend
START
Little Solsbury
Hill
Batheaston

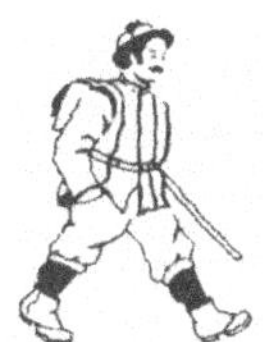

1 BATHEASTON

via Northend, Chilcombe Bottom,
Charmy Down and St Catherine's Valley

Distance:	7.5 km. 4¾ miles
Map:	Explorer 155
Map reference:	683780
Refreshments en route:	None - bring your own!

THE WALK is as varied as any in this book. Batheaston/Northend may be all but contiguous with Bath but it has a character of its own. We rapidly quit the interesting mix of buildings in the village to walk by a former reservoir, now nature reserve, then continue along Chilcombe Bottom, undisturbed but for the hum of traffic on the A46. There follows the steady ascent to Charmy Down, a plateau which served as an airfield during World War 2, then an equally steady descent to St Catherine's Valley and an enjoyable walk by a riverside path to return to Batheaston/Northend.

DIRECTIONS

To begin the walk, head north from the A4 through Batheaston towards the area known as **Northend.** Look out for the grand Eagle House on the left – its central pediment surmounted by an eagle – and Steway Lane on the right. If arriving by car there is usually somewhere to park at the roadside hereabouts.

Immediately past Eagle House turn L, passing Swinbrook Farm on your R, to reach a hedged path leading uphill. Follow this until you reach a lane. Now carry on in the same direction and continue to ascend.

Soon you will be rewarded with wide sweeping views to your right across **Ramscombe Bottom**. The lane begins to head downhill towards **Chilcombe Bottom** which once housed a reservoir to supply water for Bath.

Head for the former stone pump house and climb the steps beside it to reach the **Nature Reserve** and information board. If not too waterlogged, you can follow the beaten path to the R of the pond and stream, in the same direction you have been following, to reach an exit by a XG at the lane. Alternatively, you can follow the lane which skirts the former reservoir to the L. Both routes lead to a solitary house.

Now take the hedged path which, once again, leads you in the same direction. Follow this until it opens out, then bear L towards a gate and signposted PF and Bridleway. Take a half-R, beside the indicator post, to ascend the slope and climb the steps to reach a XG. Enjoy the view across the head of the valley to your R as you gain height. Cross here to crest the field and reach a gate. Turn R and follow the lane.

> You are now walking close to the A46 as the sounds coming from that direction will remind you.

The route is now straight ahead, climbing steadily, past **Uplands Farm** and onward until you reach the top of the slope and a junction of ways. Head directly ahead, crossing the ST beside a gate. The track now bears to the R, beside a hay barn to your L.

Go through a gate, bear R and follow the track towards the communications tower ahead. This is the perimeter road of the former airfield at **Charmy Down**. Near the tower you will reach three or four circular troughs. You now cross the end of the former runway. Follow the track between fences until you find it barred. Turn R here to pass through a XG and follow the track ahead beside a fence to your L. Change sides of the fence at the gate and ST ahead.

> You are now heading towards St Catherine's Valley. On the skyline to your L you should be able to pick out the tower of Marshfield Church beyond the Gloucestershire county boundary.

As you approach a clearing, bear R toward the stone wall, then through a gate after which the way continues as a track between stone walls and

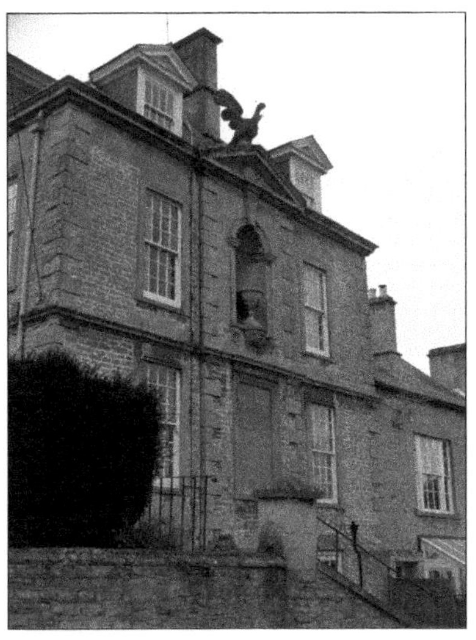

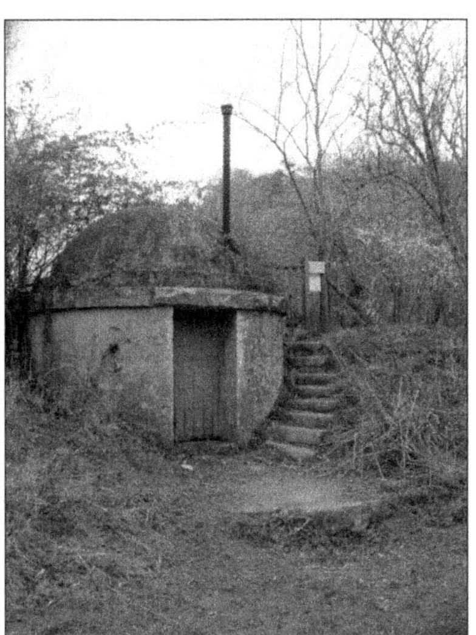

Three examples of the variety of buildings seen on the Batheaston walk:

Above left: Eagle House at Northend, dates from around 1700 but remodelled in the 1720s by John Wood the Elder who was resident here. It later became a refuge for suffragettes, including the Pankhursts, who had been released from prison following hunger strikes.

Above right: The pumping station at the former Chilcombe Bottom Reservoir which was constructed by the Bath Corporation in 1848 to provide a reliable supply of pure water for the people of Bath. Changing water quality standards and problems with leakage resulted in the reservoir being decommissioned in the 1980s. However, restoration of the site was undertaken in the mid-1990s to create a nature reserve for plants and wildlife.

Below: Anonymous blocks at the former Charmy Down airfield which was first used by the RAF from 1941 and later by the United States Air Force. It closed in 1945.

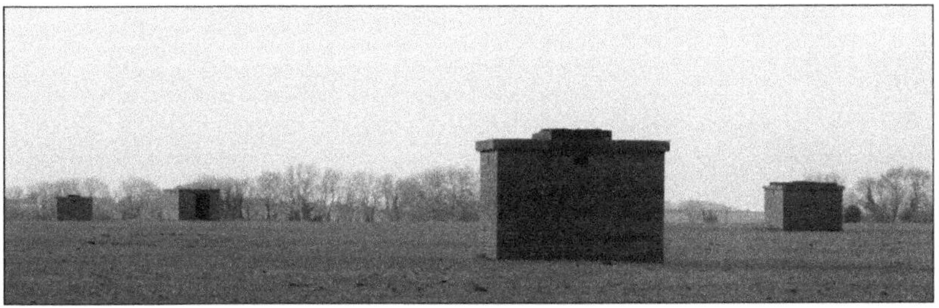

begins a gradual descent. Look out for a sharp turning on the L. Walk along here towards a bungalow called **Downedge**. On the right, just before this dwelling, is a byway heading downhill.

Follow this steepening course until you reach the lane through the valley at the entrance drive indicated **Hill Barn**. Turn L. Immediately past the house named **Valley View** on the R, look for a narrow path which you follow to descend to the buildings in the valley bottom and St Catherine's Brook.

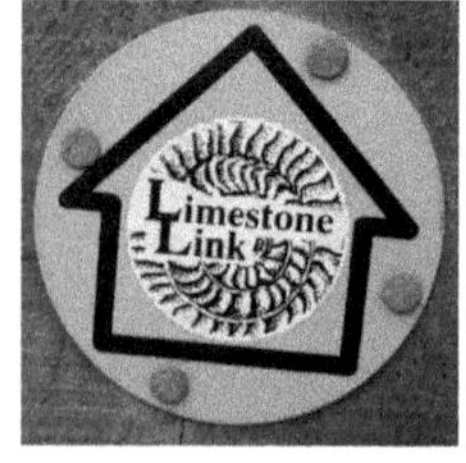

Cross over the brook and turn R to follow the route signposted **Limestone Link**. You will negotiate a succession of STs and field crossings. On reaching a lane serving Washpool water treatment works switch to the R bank by passing through a XG just past the field gate. Cross the field and, at the next field crossing, rejoin the L bank. Eventually you will see ranks of houses looming before you. Here you have reached **Steway Lane** where you turn R to find the road through Batheaston at Northend and your starting point.

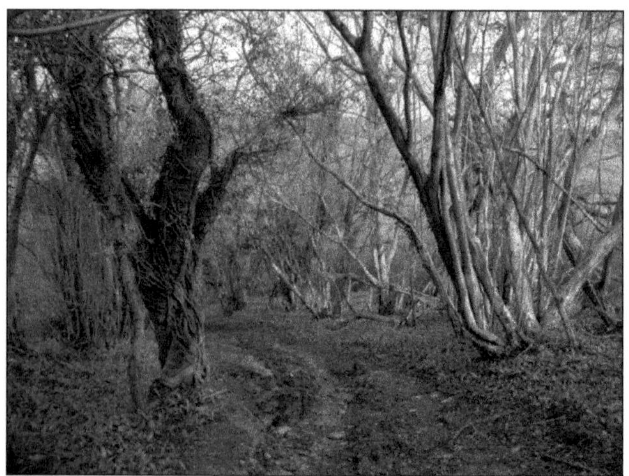

Through a wild wood on the sometimes steep
descent to St Catherine's valley and brook

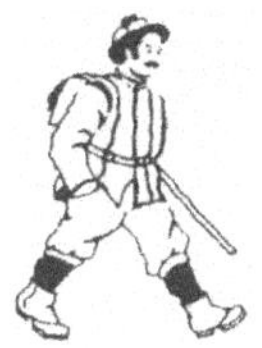

2   BATHFORD

• •

via Brown's Folly and Monkton Farleigh

Distance:	6½ km. 4 miles
Map:	Explorers 155 &156
Map reference:	669791
Refreshments en route:	Village shop and Café in Bathford;
	Kings Arms pub in Monkton Farleigh

THE WALK is without doubt located where Wiltshire meets Somerset. As its name suggests, Bathford is firmly in Somerset whilst the village of Monkton Farleigh looks across the clay vale of West Wiltshire towards Westbury White Horse, Salisbury Plain and the Vale of Pewsey. In the course of this walk, which starts with a stiff climb, we encounter a nature reserve, abandoned Bath Stone workings, an impressive nineteenth century folly and reminders of a huge former underground ammunition dump. In addition, we enjoy some exhilarating views.

DIRECTIONS

From **Church Street** bear R towards **Bathford Community Shop and Café** and carry on to the R, past the **Old Post Office and notice offering information about the village,** to reach **Dovers Park** (the bus stop is here too). Cross over and make for the track beside **No 9 Dovers Lane** which heads steadily uphill. Once past the houses it reaches a XG, reverts to a footpath and continues to rise. More houses are soon reached until you emerge onto a lane overlooked by a wooden bench to your R inscribed '**All Things Bright and Beautiful**'. Don't miss the view towards Bannerdown on your L.

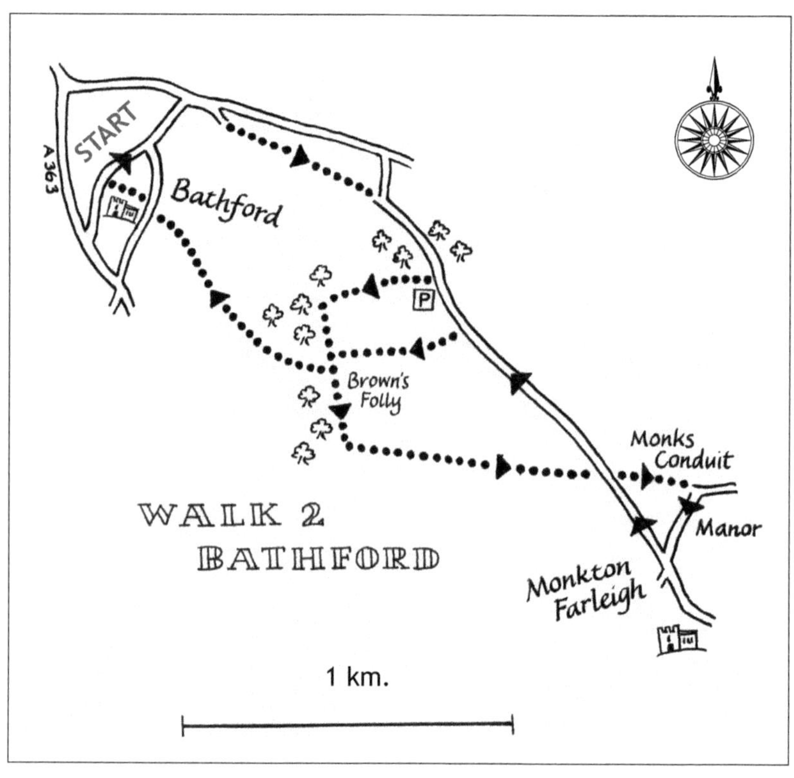

Carry on up the steeply rising lane until you reach a **car park** on the right heralding **Brown's Folly Nature Reserve**, as indicated by an information board. Now pass through the gap beside the gate to the right (not straight ahead). Follow the trail along a roughly even contour beside a steep drop to your right. You pass a second board with information relating to the former mine entrances hereabouts.

Eventually, just after taking a L fork, you reach a metal XG which leads into an open expanse offering 180 degree views to the north and west.

> This takes in Solsbury Hill, Lansdown and the well-wooded Bathampton Down, crowned with the buildings of Bath University, though details may be obscured in high summer.

Walk beneath **Brown's Folly**, also known as the Pepper Pot, until you reach a XG where the path re-enters woodland. After 200 metres or so,

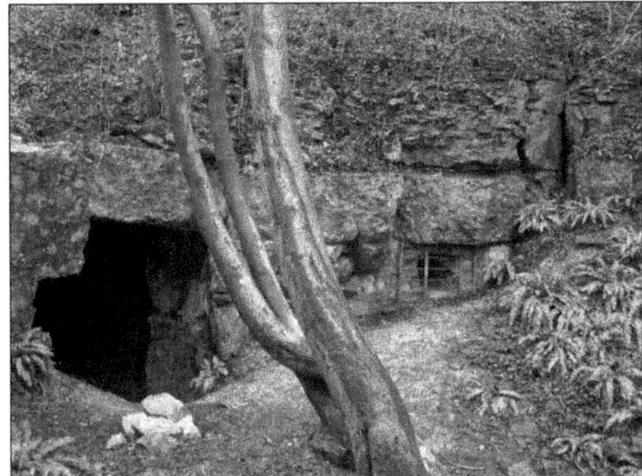

A former mine entrance at Brown's Folly Nature Reserve

Brown's Folly and some of the locals. Brown's Folly was built in 1845 by local landowner, Wade Brown, in order to provide employment for local men during the 'Hungry Forties' It bears an inscription as follows:

W 1848 B
E
C 1907 H

Presumably WB is for Wade Brown and the date 1848 for the folly's completion. CH is for Charles Hobhouse of Monkton Farleigh Manor who restored the folly in 1907

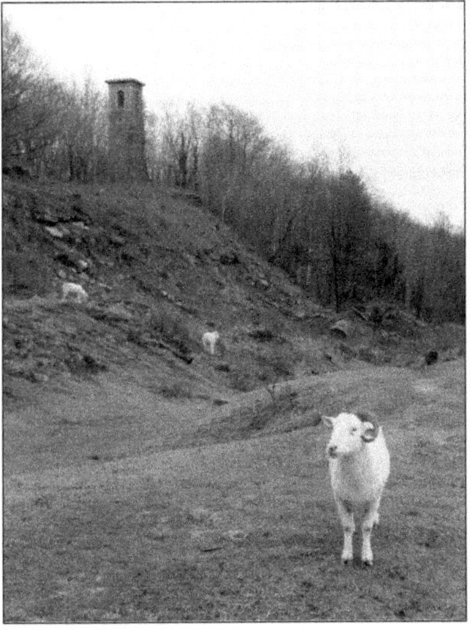

just beyond a rock which protrudes onto the path from the left, you reach a set of steps which climbs the slope to your L. Ascend here, bearing R, to reach a gap in the stone wall marked by a pair of gate posts; this marks the county boundary – you are about to leave Somerset and enter Wiltshire. Pass through the gap and continue a short distance to reach a gate marking the edge of the wood. Go through here and walk straight ahead along the field edge towards the patch of woodland ahead.

At a point where the field edge veers to the L, head straight on by the metalled drive but, almost immediately, look out for a footpath on your R which heads through the wood just to the L of a single-storey building.

You will very soon reach a lane opposite a ST which carries a PF sign. Cross over to enter a field where you proceed beside the fence on your R.

The odd-looking building you are approaching is a former boiler house and air-conditioning plant which serviced the extensive underground munitions store, inaugurated in the 1930s and finally decommissioned in 1965. This was the use to which the former Bath Stone mines were put in response to the threat of war. Follow the track as it skirts around the former plant.

A wide view opens up but is very different to that which we enjoyed just a few minutes ago. We are now looking towards Wiltshire. A particular landmark is the Westbury White Horse marking the escarpment of Salisbury Plain whilst in the foreground lies the village of Monkton Farleigh.

Cross the road ahead, then over the ST opposite and continue in the same direction towards the village along the recently created 'Jubilee Avenue'.

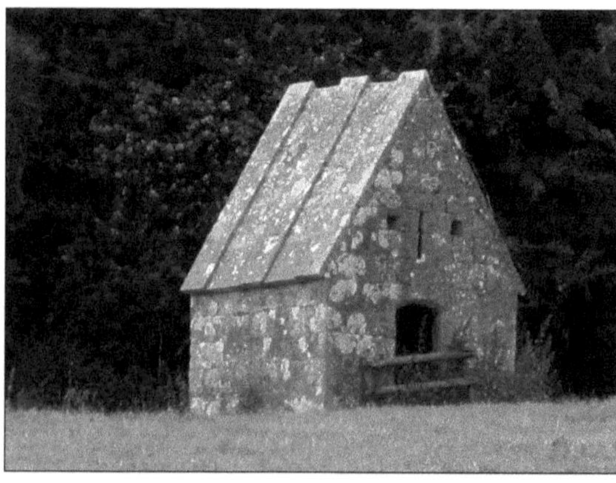

Look across the field on your R to see the **Monks Conduit**, with its steeply pitched roof, standing in solitary splendour.

You exit by a ST, beside **Home Farm**, to be confronted by the high boundary wall of Monkton Farleigh Manor.

Possible detour: Before turning R to reach the church and pub at the centre of the village, a brief detour is recommended. Carry on in the same direction to reach an indicated footpath on the L. This eventually takes you to Kingsdown but, immediately on the L there is a fenced enclosure which contains former fishponds once administered by the monks of the former monastery which predated the Manor.

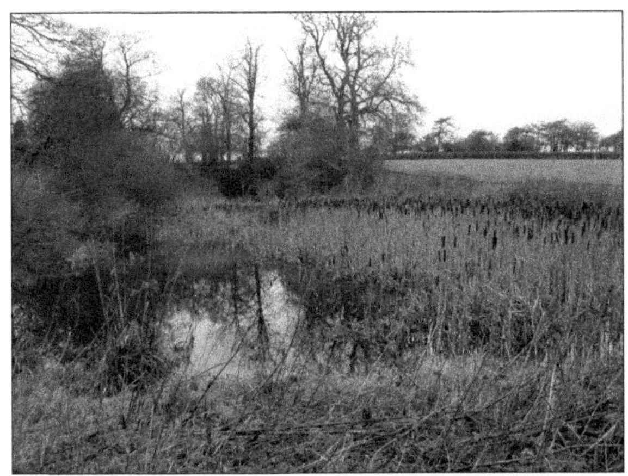

The remains of the monks' fish ponds at Monkton Farleigh

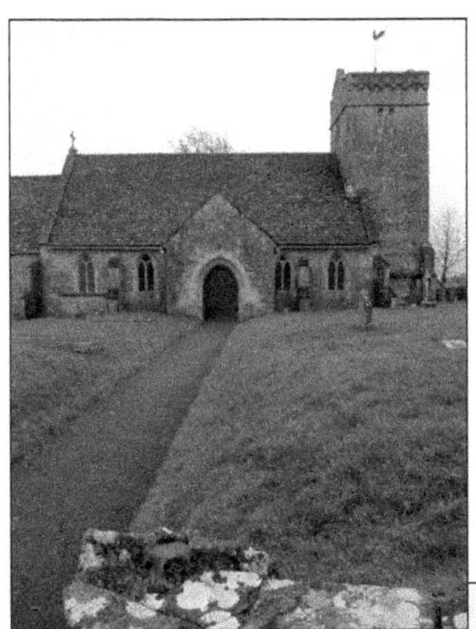

Above: As you bear right towards the Kings Arms pub in Monkton Farleigh you pass a signpost at what was once the village pump. Look out for a plate bearing the inscription WASTE NOT WANT NOT.

Monkton Farleigh: the church of St Peter

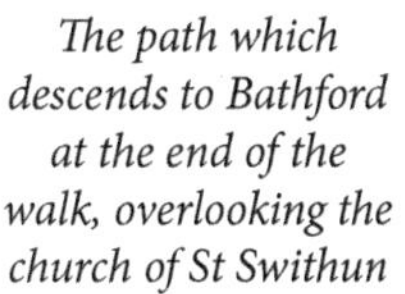

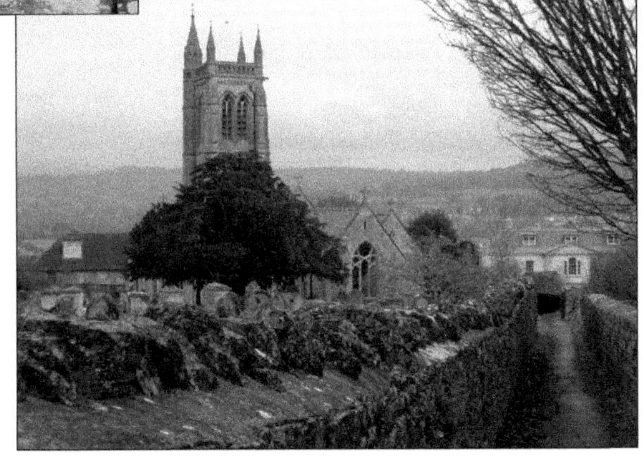

The path which descends to Bathford at the end of the walk, overlooking the church of St Swithun

To continue the walk: facing **Home Farm**, bear L towards the village. When you reach the main street you will find the pub to your R and the church away to your L.

To complete the walk back to Bathford you head up the lane, past the pub. Pass a couple of entrances to works on your L. Then, just beyond a lane signposted to Bath on your R, look out for a permissive path on your L. Enter here and keep following the yellow direction arrows, bearing L by the edge of the wood until you reach the foot of **Brown's Folly** where you will enjoy stunning views towards Bath and its surrounding hills.

Descend by the rough steps from Brown's Folly, keeping to the L. You will reach the XG which you encountered earlier. Now repeat your previous footsteps for 200 metres or so, not quite as far as the protruding rock and the staircase which you climbed earlier but to a point where a footpath sets off sharply to your R to follow a diagonal course downhill.

This leads you to a wider track; follow this for just a few yards, then peel off by a continuation of the path to the L – indicated **Public Foorpath**. Continue the descent to reach a ST and information board. Here you leave the Nature Reserve to be rewarded with a final inspiring view across an open field to Bath (see below) and, closer to hand, the tower of Bathford church, a fitting finale to your ramble.

Cross the ST to exit the field, bear L, then R and look out for the indicated PF to the L beside **Manor Farm Cottage**. Now descend by a walled path to reach the church. From here bear R along Church Street to reach the main road where you turn R towards the Community shop and café.

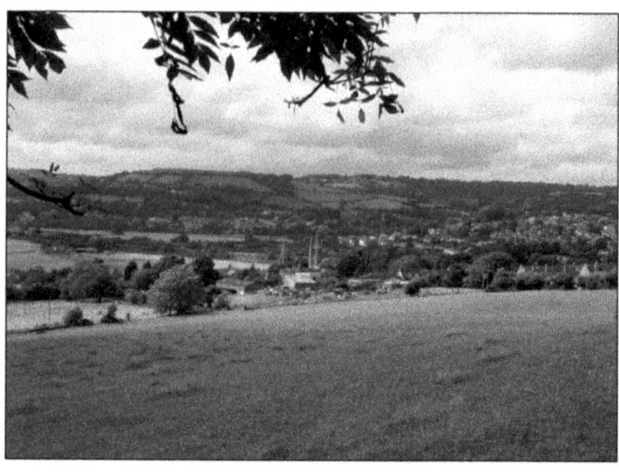

One of many fine view-points; this one crossing a field back to Bathford on the last leg of the walk

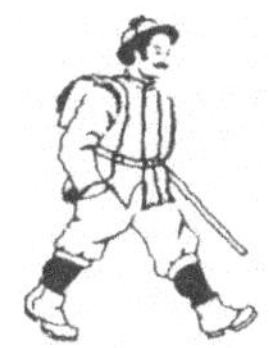

3 BOX

via Colerne and Ditteridge

Distance:	8.5 km. 5¼ miles
Map:	Explorer 156
Map reference:	685825
Refreshments en route:	Pubs and cafés in Box and Colerne

THE WALK, though not a long one, does include a fair amount of upping and downing: there is a steady climb from the By Brook to Colerne on the edge of Bannerdown which, like Charmy Down and Lansdown to the west, is an elevated plateau. Following Colerne's level High Street, there is a steady descent to the tributary Lid Brook, then a short and sharp ascent before a final downward slope via the hamlet of Ditteridge and return to Box.

DIRECTIONS

From the top of **Valens Terrace**, before beginning the walk it is worth heading back up to the main road where you will find **Box Blind House**, an historic lock up, a few yards along to the L, and the **church of Thomas à Becket** down **Church Lane** to the R.

To begin the walk: Facing downhill from the top of **Valens Terrace**, look out for the PF on the R. Follow a diagonal course across the playing field to a point in the lower R-hand corner. Alternatively, if you have parked in the free car park at the bottom of Valens Terrace, head straight across the playing field to the far L corner.

To your R you will see the higher ground of Box Hill, through which Brunel excavated a tunnel, almost two miles in length, for the GWR.

1 km.
Colerne
Lid Brook
WALK 3
BOX
Ditteridge
Middlehill
Box
By Brook
START

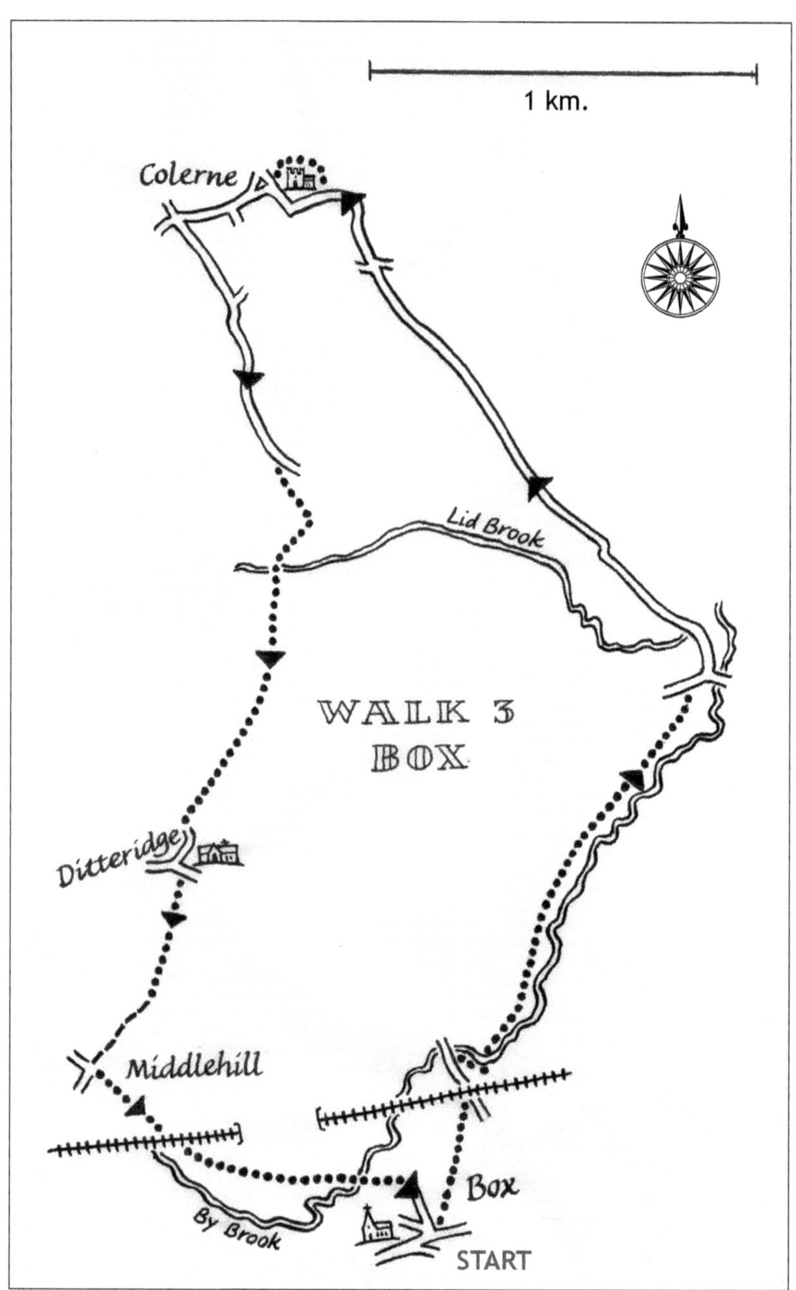

24

There is a stream flowing to the L and the embankment of the railway main line beyond. Bear R to reach Mill Lane where you turn L through a tunnel beneath the railway. Ignore the PF immediately on your R but carry on for a short distance to reach a bridge over the **By Brook**. <u>Do not cross over</u> but look out for a PF on your R, also indicated as the **Macmillan Way**. Cross a wooden bridge and pass the outfall of the mill stream to your R.

Follow the fenced path, then pass through a XG to head across a couple of low-lying fields which border the By Brook. Pass through a metal XG and then, as you approach the end of the second field, bear a little uphill and to the L to reach a wooden XG leading to a second one. From here you will spot the tower of **Colerne church** on the skyline ahead. Turn R and then L up the lane past **Saltbox Farm**. There is a steady climb ahead. You eventually reach a fork: don't bear L but head straight on.

You pass a canopied former well. As you reach the village keep your eyes peeled for a wooden gate on the R signposted 'Consecrated Grounds'. Enter the churchyard here, with its several fine specimen trees, for an attractive short cut to the church entrance. Note the fine cross inscribed with Celtic knotwork and the bench with its memorial plate.

Exit the churchyard into Market Place and head along the High Street, past the **Six Bells** pub on the R. Further along you will reach the **Fox and Hounds** pub.

The next stage of the walk begins by descending **Ogbourne** which is found past **Six Bells** pub but before the **Fox and Hounds** and almost opposite **Silver Street**. Just past the house named **South View Cottage** there is a PF indicated to the L. This is a narrow, walled path which soon becomes a tunnel overhung with trees on both sides.

You reach a lane where you continue to descend. Ignore the first PF on the right but, just past a L-hand bend, look out for a ST on the R, close to a stables. Cross here and head a little to the R to the next ST. Walk straight on and, once over the ridge, you descend the slope to reach a gate and bridge across the stream flowing to the L below. This is the Lid Brook wending its way to join the By Brook. The PF sign here will inform that you have now joined the **Palladian Way**, bound for Bath.

Now climb the slope with the hedgerow to your R. Cross a wooden step ST, next a squeezer ST. Continue in the same direction by following the hedgerow to your L until the view opens out.

Ashley is straight ahead with Box to its left but closer to hand is the hamlet of **Ditteridge** – the nave and bell tower of its ancient **St Christopher** church is just below.

Head through a squeezer ST to exit the field, then through the gate immediately on your L which leads into the churchyard. Leave the churchyard on the far side and walk down the lane to the T-junction. Look for the PF just to the L of **The Bungalow**.

Carry on down and across the field to reach a step ST at the bottom. Follow the drive to the R, passing **Spa House**, to reach a junction below. Cross over and bear L by the indicated PF. Pass **Meadowbrook Cottage** and continue by a fenced path, across a ST, through the tunnel under the railway and through a gate into an open field. You can now see the slender spire of Box church ahead.

Pass through a XG. Follow the beaten path to the L, below the slope, until you reach a stoutly constructed XG. Once through here, follow the path across a stone bridge, then turn R and descend to cross a wooden footbridge and bear R. You reach a circular moated island which you follow in a clockwise direction. At about 10 o'clock climb the staircase to reach a corner of the playing field and your starting point.

Here you will discover the **Box Rock Circus** – a splendid geological exhibit which was unveiled in 2013. There is a helpful information panel explaining the geological succession and how the rocks displayed relate to it.

The car park is nearby and the High Street at the top of Valens Terrace

Church of St Christopher,
Ditteridge

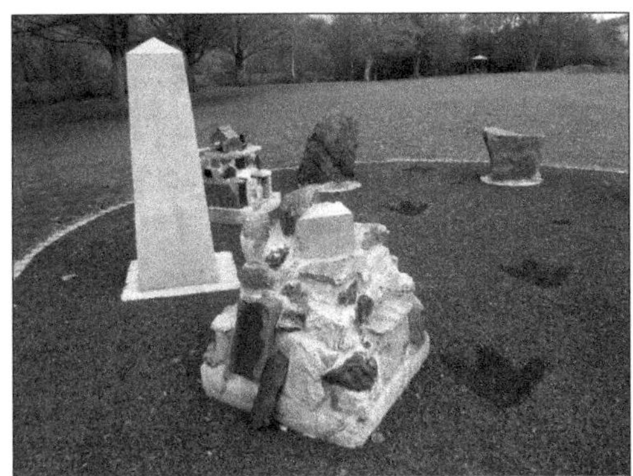

Clockwise from top left:

The Palladian Way which is joined briefly at Lid Brook;

The Rock Circus at Box;

Riders heading towards Colerne

Dedication on bench in Colerne churchyard;

Celtic cross in churchyard;

Roofed well in Colerne

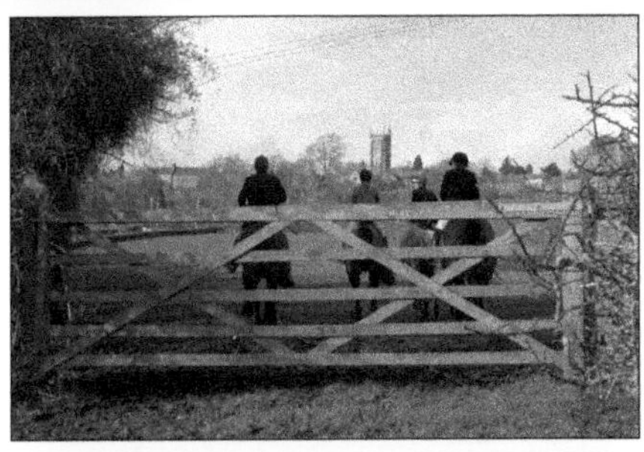

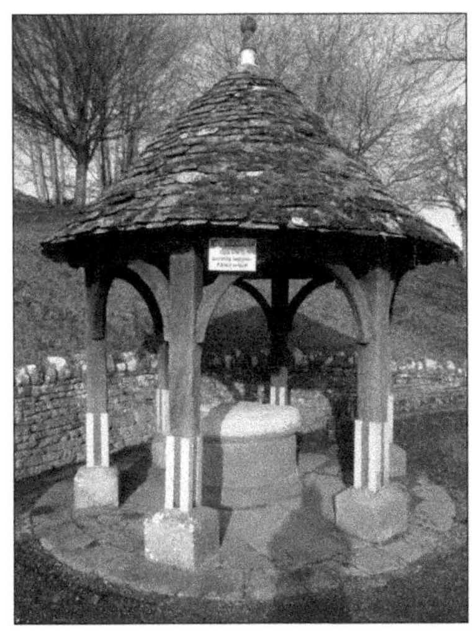

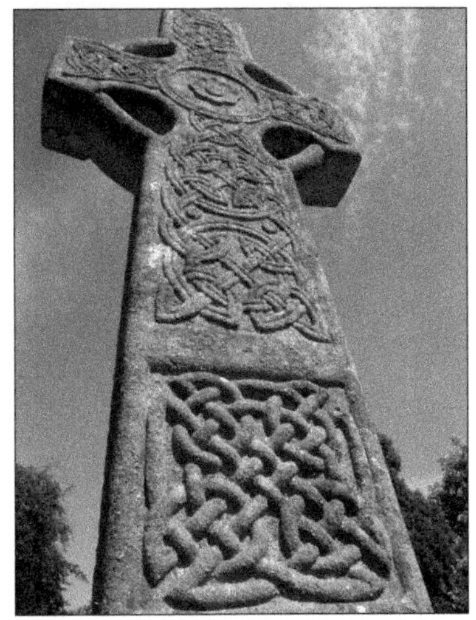

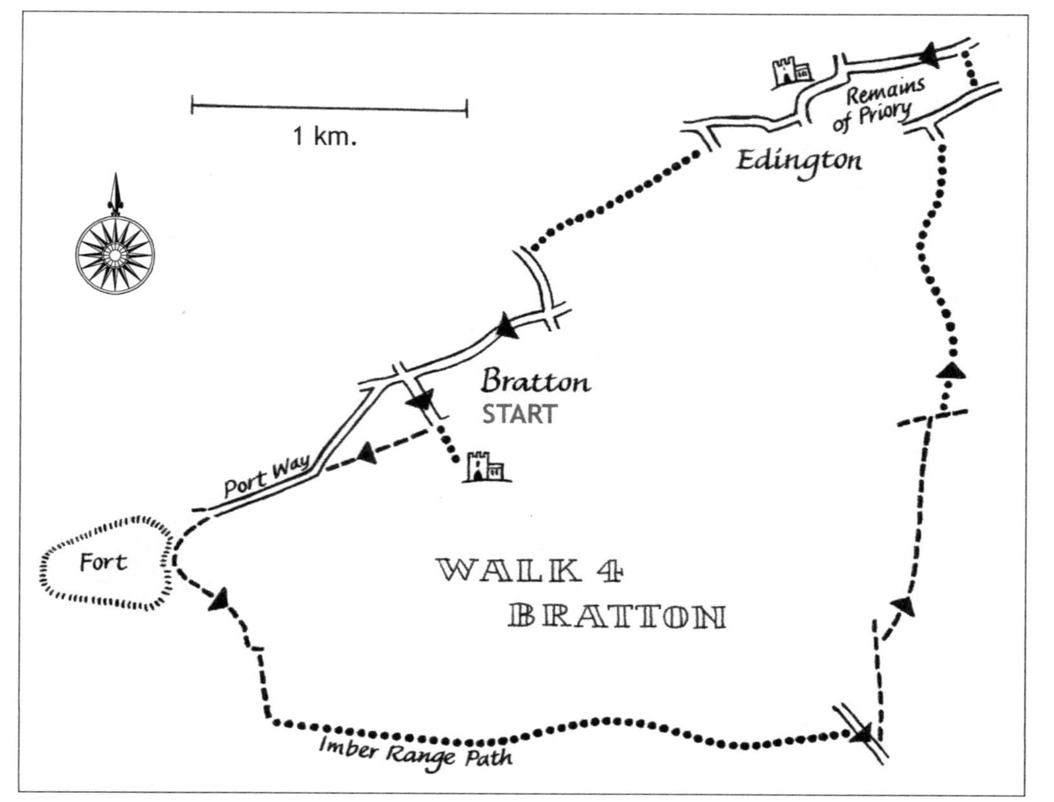

1 km.
Remains
of Priory
Edington
Bratton
START
Port Way
Fort
WALK 4
BRATTON
Imber Range Path

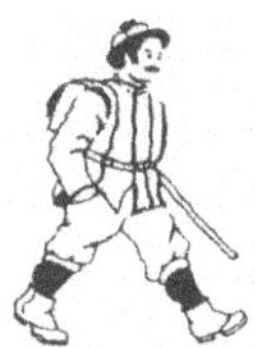

4 BRATTON

via Imber Range Perimeter Path and Edington

Distance:	10½ km 6½ miles
Map:	Explorer 143
Map Reference:	523916
Refreshments en route:	The Duke pub in Bratton; also village shop. The Three Daggers pub and farm shop in Edington.

THE WALK is a good stretch. There is a steady but not overly steep ascent at the outset after which the route is pretty much on the level. We follow the Imber Range Perimeter Path for some distance, which marks the boundary of the Army Firing Ranges and affords some fine views across the sweeping downland on the edge of Salisbury Plain and, in the other direction, across the clay vale to the Devizes Downs beyond. A change of direction leads to a sharp descent to reach Edington and finally across fields to return to Bratton. There is plenty of interest in both Bratton and Edington, the two villages visited.

DIRECTIONS

From the centre of **Bratton**, in the vicinity of the green, the Duke pub, Hillside Stores and Jubilee Hall, begin by heading west along Westbury Road, past **Carpenters Lane** on your R, then turn L, opposite **Court Lane**, via the PF sign indicating ¼ mile to the Church. You reach a junction of tracks where you turn R.

Possible detour: To reach the church, rather remote from the village, follow the flight of steps ahead. These descend to a stream fed by springs at the foot of the combe just to the right. Climb up to reach the church.

Back at the junction and facing in the direction of the church, turn R along the track signposted as Bridleway to Bratton Castle. Once past the houses along here, the track soon narrows but eventually reaches the **Port Way** which climbs towards Bratton Castle and Westbury White Horse.

The view opens up as you reach the road: the former cement works are fairly close by to the L and the Devizes Downs in the distance to the R. Bear L and begin climbing but look out for an indicated **Bridleway** L and R. Bear L and follow the track as it curves around the head of The Combe. This is a stunningly sculpted dry valley; the tower of Bratton Church amid trees is visible at its foot. You should also be able to identify the tower of Edington Church in the distance.

Carry on to pass a ST on your right. When you reach a farm gate and ST go through the gate and head straight on along the sunken way. Two more gates will take you onto a well-made track signposted as the **Imber Range Path**. Turn L here and follow the way for some 2½ kilometres or 1½ miles. You should be able to pick out the tower of Steeple Ashton church in the clay vale to your L.

To continue: you will gradually descend towards a group of farm buildings until you reach a T-junction. Turn R here. You will spot the entrance gate to the **Imber Army Ranges** ahead. Here turn very sharp L along a grassy enclosed track. This follows the route of the Wessex Rodgeway though it is not indicated at this juncture. When the track forks, bear R with the buildings of Westdown Farm away to the R.

You reach a barn – here is a red windsock bearing the name 'Turnip Airways' – where you bear R and immediately L. You descend gradually to meet a farm gate. Once through here you encounter a recently constructed corral. Note the memorial plate attached to a piece of timber. Now bear R to reach a gate and follow the way ahead beyond the corral: this descending path becomes steeper and more sunken as you approach **Edington** village.

At the road turn R. There is no pavement here so it is advisable to keep well in on the R-hand side until you spot the pavement on the far side when you should cross with care. Here you come to the impressive **Edington Farm Shop** and, just beyond, the **Three Daggers pub**.

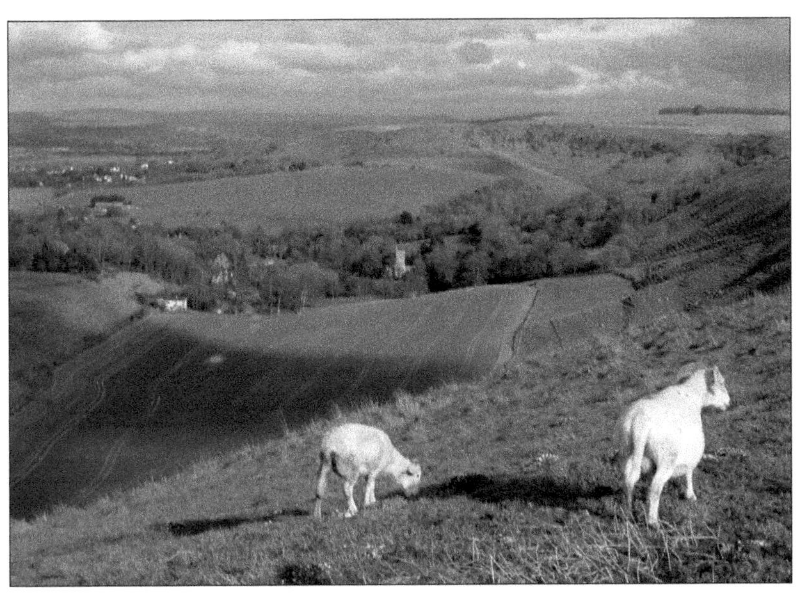

Spring and summer views down Bratton Combe.
The tower of Bratton Church, amid trees, is visible in both

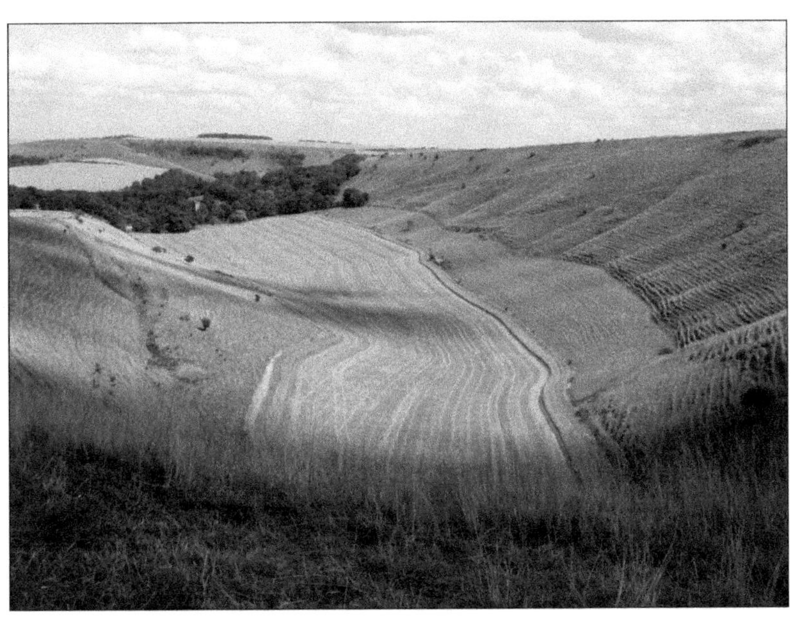

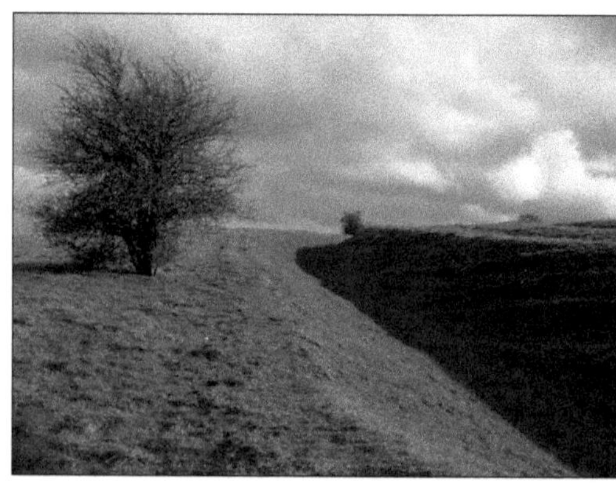

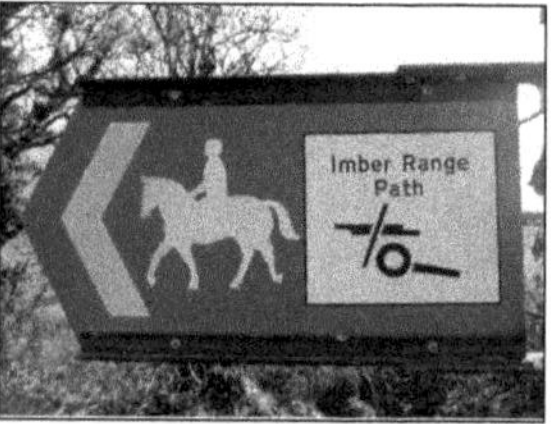

*Sunken way
leading to
Imber Range
Path*

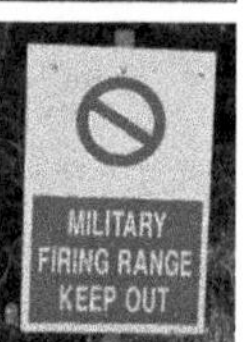

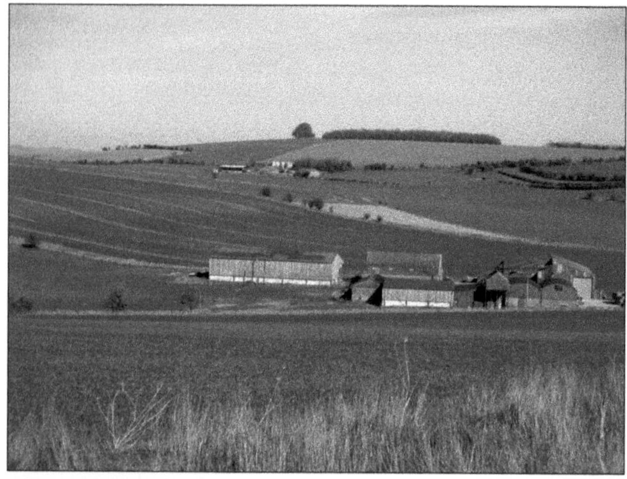

Reeves Farm with, in the distance, Westdown Farm, seen from the Imber Range Path

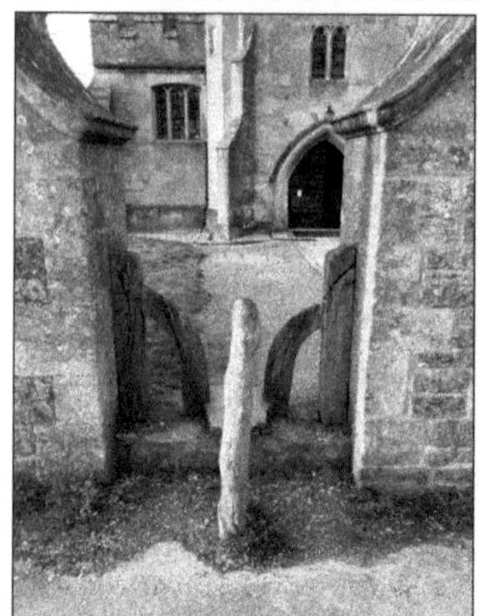

Post and stile at the entrance to Edington Church

Sign indicating Ralph's Seat, named for Ralph Dudley, a former vicar of Edington Priory who founded the Friends of Edington in 1956 at a time when the church fabric was in urgent need of repair. The first Choir Festival, which became the Music Festival, was held the same year

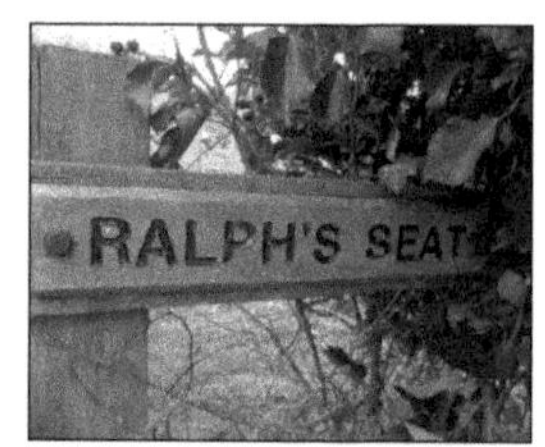

Immediately past the pub, turn L down the signposted footpath, beside two bungalows, Nos 4 and 4A, on the L and a **pond** on the R, to meet a lane joining from the R. Now turn L by the **post box** along a metalled path. Carry on past houses until you reach a high stone wall. Here bear L and R to reach **Edington Church**.

You will find steps which ascend the hillock opposite the entrance to the church to reach Ralph's Seat, a climb worth taking, not so much for the view of the church, which is generally obscured by trees, but the view in the opposite direction to the chalk escarpment which looms above the village looking like a tsunami about to engulf it.

Walk through the churchyard and exit by a gate to the L. Now follow the gravelled path to reach a lane where you bear L, then R where a road joins from the L. Continue in the same direction. Once past the last house on your L you turn L along **Greater Lane**.

Very soon look out for a PF sign to Bratton on your R. Go through the XG and climb up to a further XG to follow the hedgerow on your R. A further XG will lead you to a narrow path which descends to a stream and **The Old Mill**.

On reaching the lane, cross over and carry on by the path opposite. This enclosed way will eventually lead you to the war memorial on the road through Bratton and your starting point.

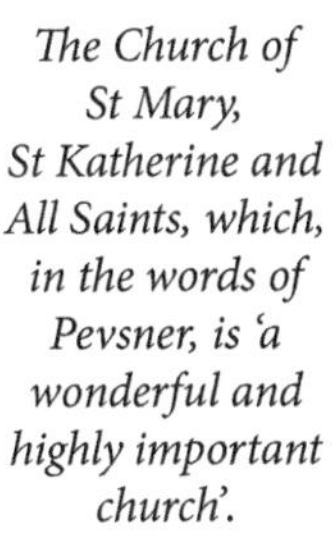

The Church of St Mary, St Katherine and All Saints, which, in the words of Pevsner, is 'a wonderful and highly important church'.

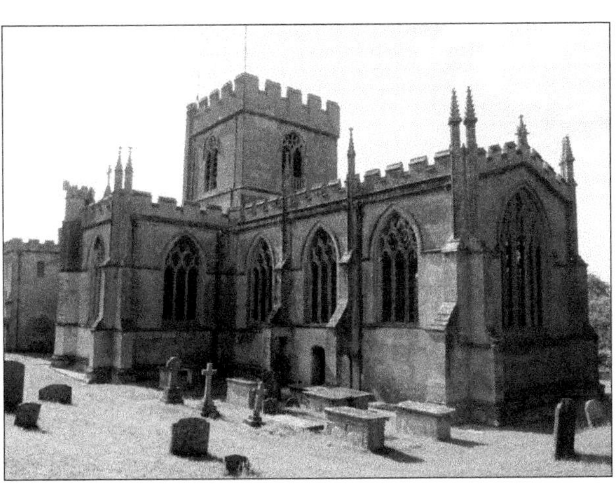

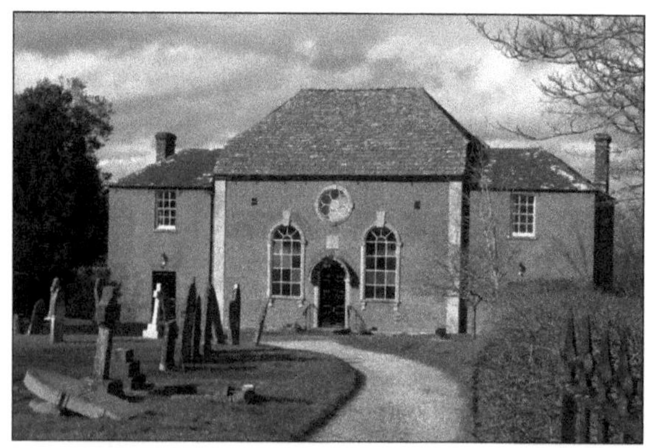

Bratton's attractive Baptist church dating from 1734

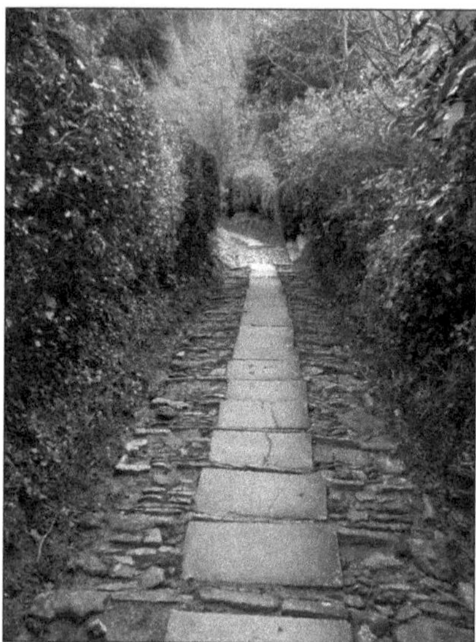

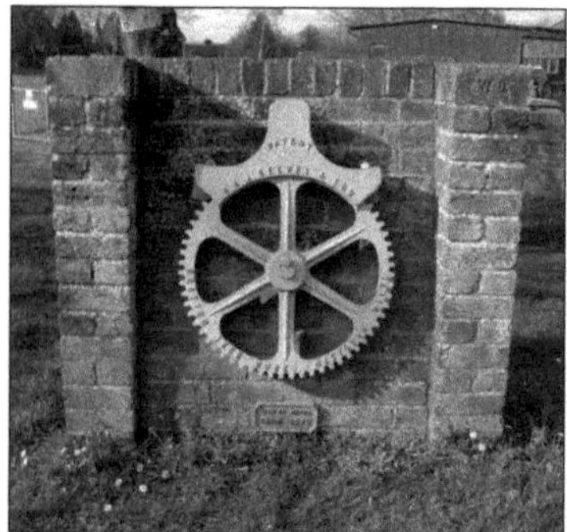

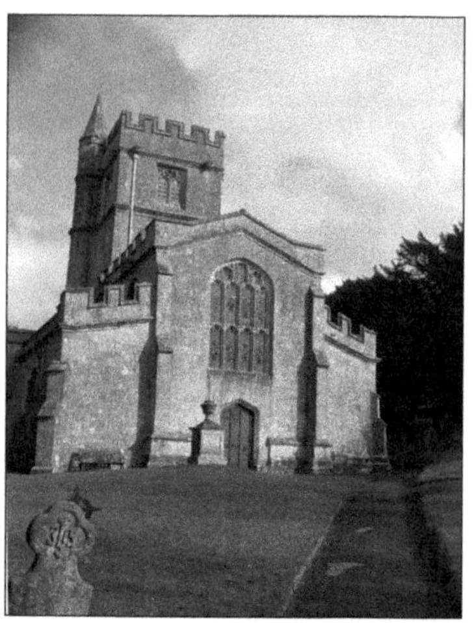

Above left: The path which leads down to a stream and up again to reach St James Church in Bratton. Like Edington, Bratton is a springline village, its vital water supply provided by springs which emanate from the junction of the porous chalk and greensand strata with impervious clay.

Above right: Monument commemorating Reeves Iron Works which manufactured all manner of agricultural implements and was a major village enterprise.

St James Church

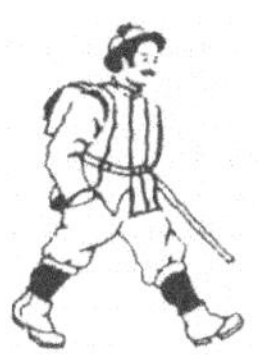

5 BROUGHTON GIFFORD

via Great Chalfield, Holt, Staverton and Whaddon

Distance	11½ km. 7¼ miles
Parking:	There is generally a space to pull in close to The Bell on the Common
Map:	Explorer 156
Map reference:	641875
Refreshments en route:	The Bell on the Common in Broughton Gifford; the Ham Tree Inn, the Tollgate Inn, the Field Kitchen and Rose Garden Tea Room at The Courts in Holt; the Bear in Staverton. Shop in Holt.

THE WALK is a longish one – it took me 2½ hours the last time I tackled it, but with only brief stops to take in the views. As reward, however, it is pretty much on the level with few ups and downs, through open fields and beside the River Avon. En route are three villages which offer no fewer than five pubs, plus an excellent café in Holt. There are two National Trust properties: the manor at Great Chalfield and The Courts in Holt; the latter offering its Rose Garden Tea Room. If you intend to include a stop at either of these sites, be sure to check opening times.

NOTE: As you approach Staverton there is an unavoidable stretch of walking beside a road where extra care should be taken.

DIRECTIONS

From **The Bell on the Common** head along the southern perimeter of **The Common**. As you reach the far corner you will spot a PF sign pointing L. Follow the rough track here until you reach a field. Follow the hedge on

---

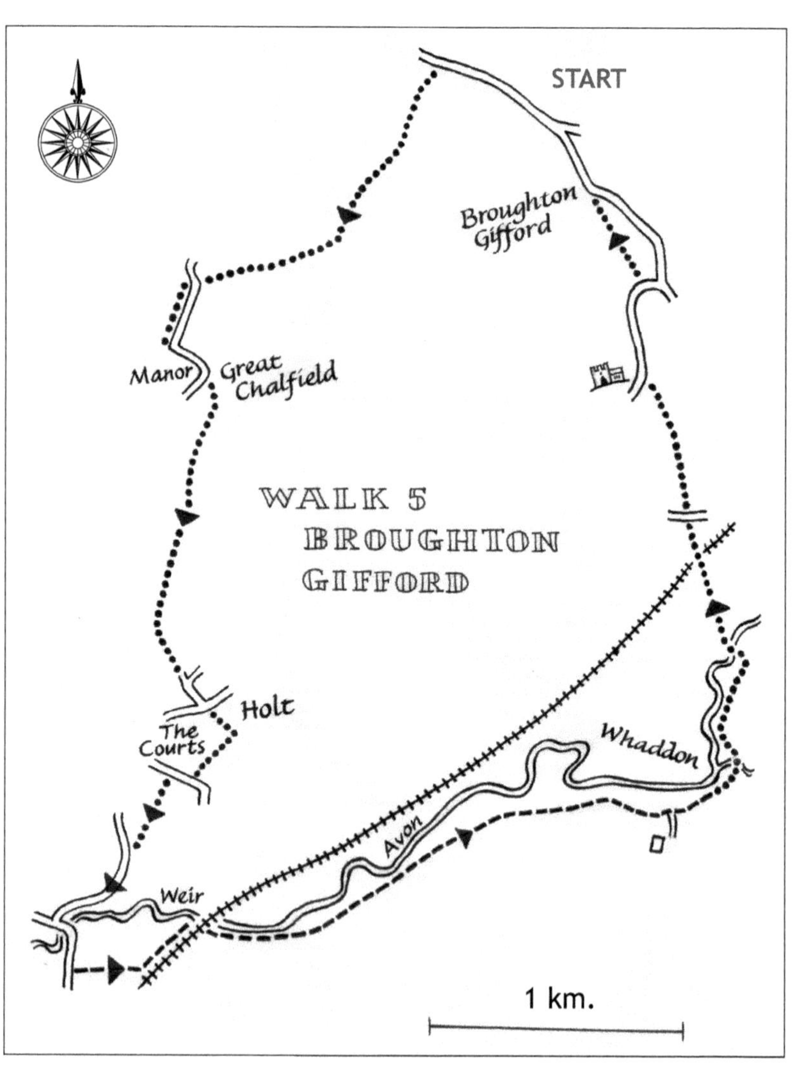

START
Broughton
Gifford
Manor
Great
Chalfield
WALK 5
BROUGHTON
GIFFORD
Holt
The
Courts
Weir
Avon
Whaddon
1 km.

your R. Cross into one field, then another. Keep your eyes peeled for a crossing to your R where you negotiate a bridge across a ditch to enter an open field with a view beyond (when the trees are not in leaf) towards Great Chalfield.

Follow the beaten path here to reach the next field, then in the same direction to reach another. Rather than heading straight on, bear a little to the R to leave this field at a point near a far corner to reach a lane.

This is a slight detour but it is worth walking this lane to enjoy a gradual approach to the range of ancient buildings with comprise **Great Chalfield**.

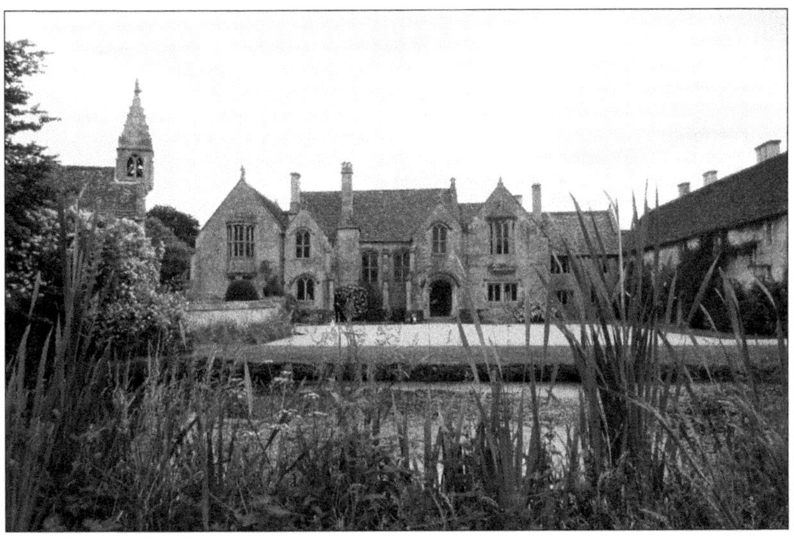

Great Chalfield Manor and the tiny church of All Saints to the left

On reaching the manor house complex, bear L to follow the moated boundary until you reach a gate at a point where the lane takes a R-turn. Enter the field here and descend to a footbridge. Follow the hedgerow on your L through one field crossing, then another. You will see the buildings of **Holt** village ahead. Descend to a third crossing. Once through here look out for a XG <u>almost immediately on your R</u>, which may be all but obscured in high summer.

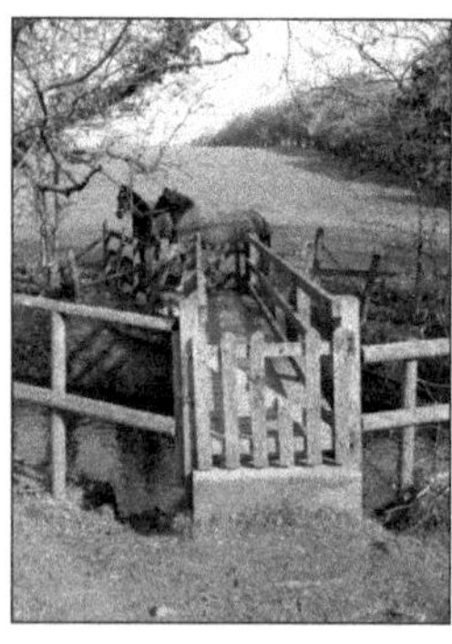

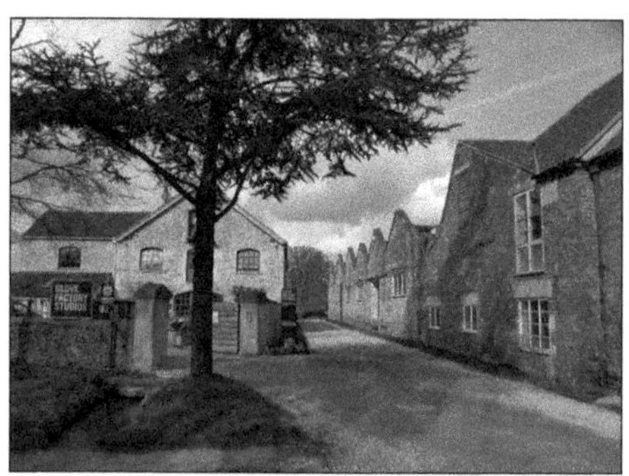

Clockwise from above left: Gated bridge across stream below Great Chalfield

The former Glove Factory in Holt, now the Glove Factory Studios

Monumental stone-roofed bench on Holt village green

The Courts, described by Pevsner in his Wiltshire volume as follows: 'An early C18 façade of five bays, wildly overdone in all its details, an instructive example of what a vulgar mind can do with mising elements.'

Sign in wall of Holt village hall stating its original purpose

St Katherine's church, Holt

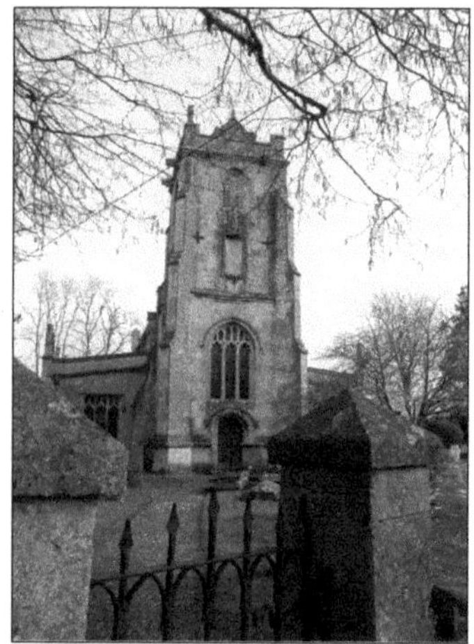

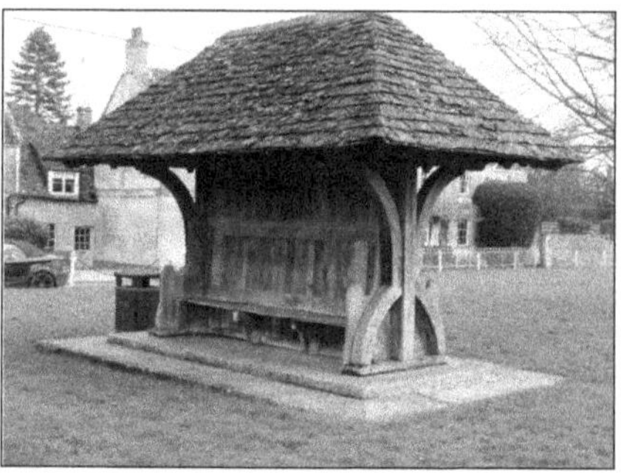

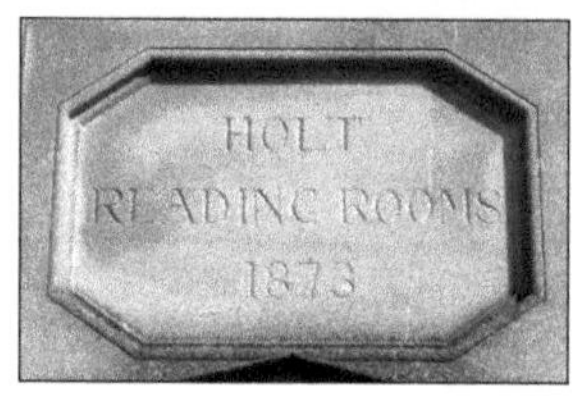

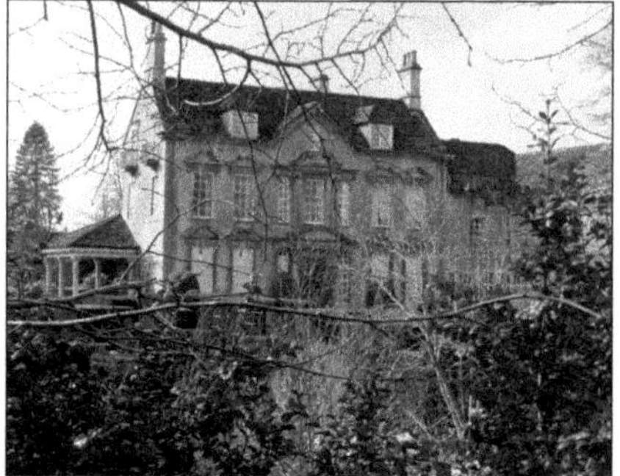

Follow the field boundary with the hedgrow to your L. This eventually curves to the R. Continue beside the wire fence until you reach a XG. Now bear L and follow the fenced path beside the field boundary, through a right angle to reach a driveway. This heads through the industrial buildings of the former Glove Factory, converted into the **Glove Factory Studios** where you will find The Field Kitchen.

Head on past **Holt Village Hall** to reach the main road through the village. Cross over directly, past the entrance to the National Trust property known as **The Courts** and along the track signposted PF. You reach an old iron squeezer ST - go through here and turn R to follow the boundary of the gardens of The Courts. You will soon reach the lane with the former village school opposite; turn R beside **St Katherine's church**. (Holt's two pubs may be found by walking straight on.)

Walk past **New Holt Cemetery** and look out for the PF sign on the L. Head across the field to reach the ST below. The prospect now is towards the uncompromising bulk of the works at **Staverton**. Cross a ST in the hedgerow below and exit this field by a ST in the hedgerow on the R. There is a short distance to walk along this narrow lane which can often be quite busy, so take care. You will soon spot the River Avon to your L.

At the junction turn L, across the river and past the industrial buildings, once a water-powered woollen mill, now the works of CPW (Cereal Partners Worldwide). Head past the drive into the works and you will see, to your R, the entrance to **St Paul's Church**.

This church has been declared redundant but offers views over the River Avon as it wends its course via Great Bradford Wood towards Bradford on Avon. If you do venture here notice the grand iron gates at the entrance which were fashioned by the Coalbrookdale Company. The Old Bear Inn is a little further along the road on the R and former Wesleyan Chapel, 1824.

Turn L, just before the former Wesleyan Chapel, dated 1824, via the signposted bridleway past the terrace of three cottages known as **NASMILCO**.

This is an acronym which stands for Nestlés Anglo Swiss Milk Company,

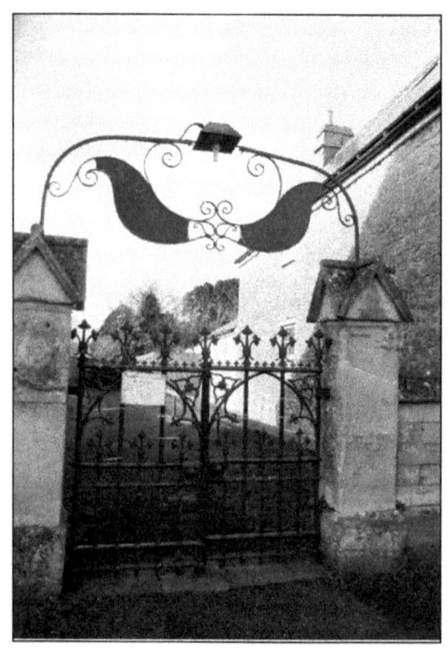

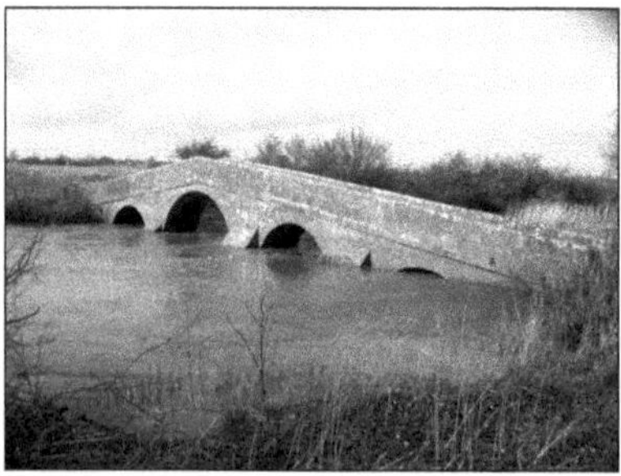

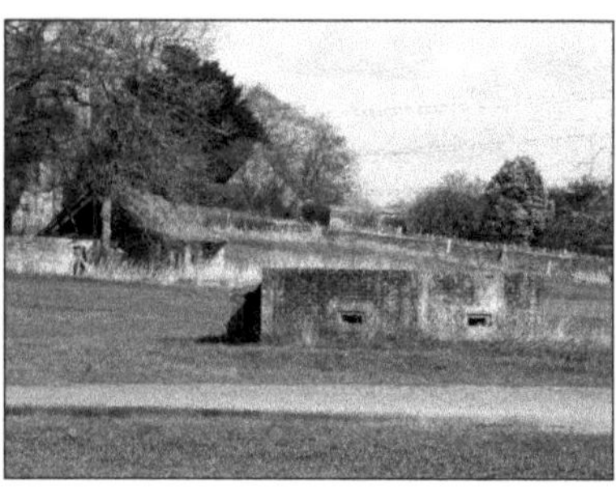

Clockwise from above left:

Iron entrance gates leading to the redundant church of St Paul's, Staverton

Whaddon packhorse bridge

Pillbox beside the Avon

Sign of the Bell on the Common pub in Broughton Gifford

St Mary's church, Whaddon

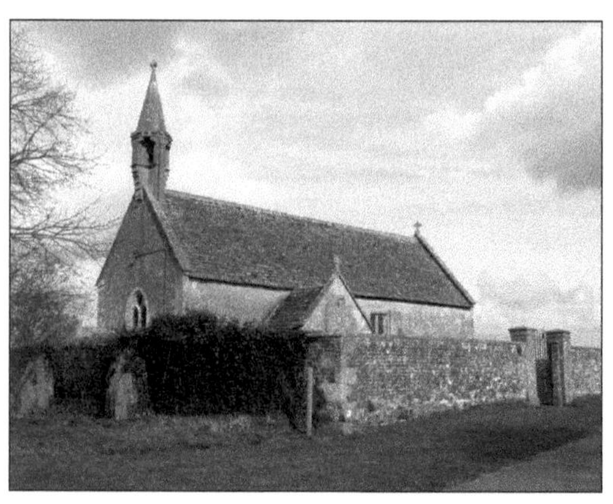

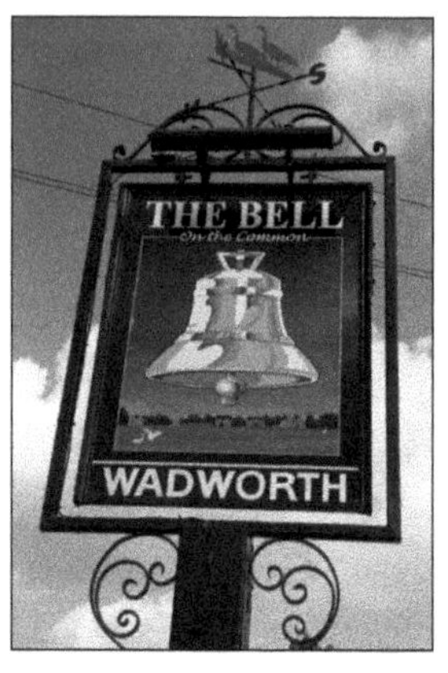

Nestlés being a former occupier of the factory here. When the road bears L into the works car park, head straight on by the fenced footpath to follow the works perimeter and savour the malty odour.

Pass beneath the railway bridge beside the Avon and reach a gate leading into a field. Look out for a path descending to your L to cross a ditch and continue beside the Avon. Similarly, keep your eyes peeled for a concealed crossing on your L. Don't descend to towards the river but head straight on beside an extensive solar array to your R and above what appears to be an extended shepherd's hut below. Now simply follow the beaten path ahead through three more field crossings towards the farm and little church of St Mary's at **Whaddon** whose belfry, surmounted by a miniature spire, soon comes into view.

As you approach the church in its walled enclosure you will see a PF sign pointing L. Follow this direction around the far side of the church and then bear L between a pair of fenced trees, down a slope to reach a ST. Cross over and head on to the elegant little footbridge across the Avon's tributary Semington Brook. Bear L across the field towards the Avon once again to find the next field beyond the former pier of an old railway bridge which once crossed the river here and on towards Devizes. You will now spot the old **packhorse bridge** ahead.

Cross over - observe the Second World War pillbox away to the right. Head up to the next ST, cross another field and another ST to reach a railway track. Stop, Look, Listen and when all is clear cross over. Next up is a road so the same drill. Cross the next field by heading towards the tower of **Broughton Gifford's St Mary's Church** and to the R of a bungalow until you spot a bridge and ST. Another XG leads you beside the cemetery to join the road.

Bear R, past the primary school, and look out for a PF sign, gate and ST on your L. Cross the field by the beaten path to exit by a ST to rejoin the road. Bear L once again, past the war memorial to reach your starting point at The Bell on the Common.

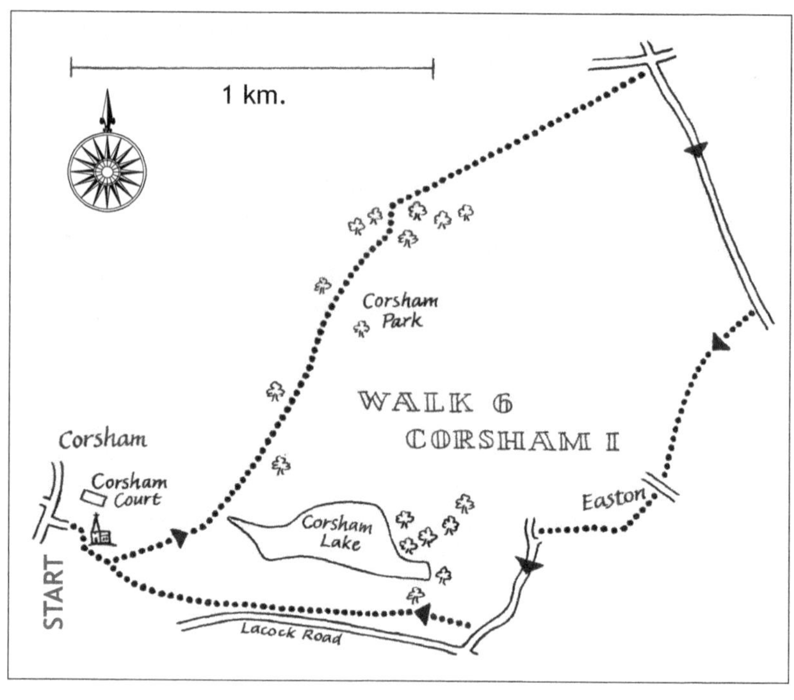

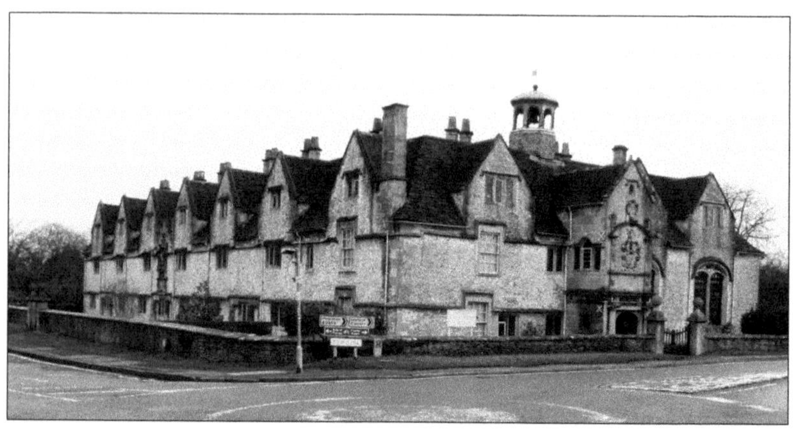

The Hungerford Almshouses, not directly on the route of this walk but close by and worth seeking out.

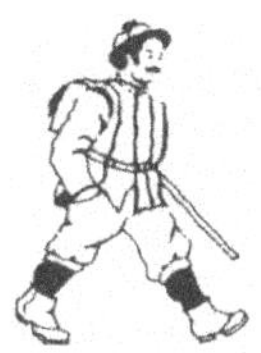

6   CORSHAM 1

via Corsham Park

Distance:	5½ km. 3½ miles
Map:	Explorer 156
Map reference:	705874
Refreshments en route:	The usual range of fcilities in Corsham

THE WALK is an easy, well signposted one, all on the level around parkland and across fields to the east of Corsham Court.

DIRECTIONS

From Corsham's **High Street**, head down **Church Street**, past the **sham ruin** to reach the car park and the distant façade of **Corsham Court** to your L.

There is a useful bird's eye plan of the town posted here which is worth viewing before entering the grounds of St Bartholomew's church with its soaring spire.

From the entrance porch head across the churchyard to reach an old iron XG. Once through here bear L to follow the beaten path beside the boundary of the churchyard and the grounds of Corsham Court – clearly identified by the ha ha. Pass through an iron XG and continue to follow the ha ha. You will soon catch a glimpse of the lake in the R distance.

At the second XG and '**Please Keep to Public Footpath**' sign eventually bear a little to the R and head towards a modern steel XG, then through a belt of woodland and over a rustic stone bridge. Once more bear a little to the R to follow the path to the R of a number of mature oak trees.

You will now be aware of the main road, the A4, which runs along the

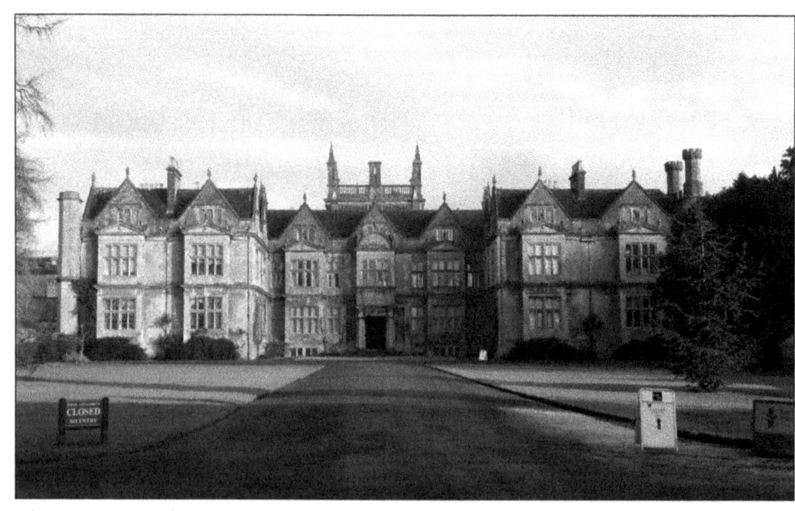

The impressive if not quite symmetrical façade of Corsham Court which dates back to the Elizabethan age but was remodelled, together with the grounds, by Capability Brown in the 1760s

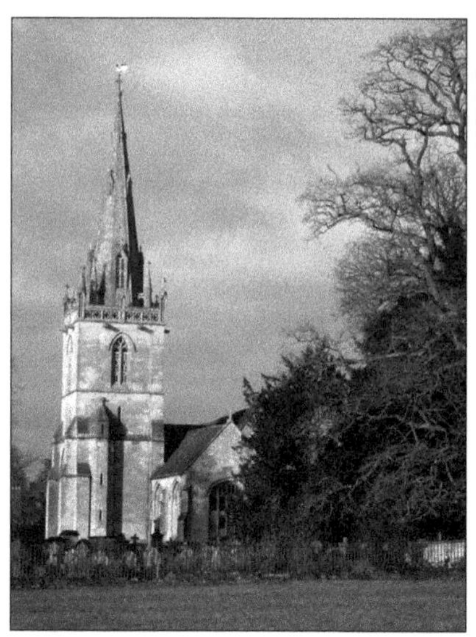

The sham ruin built in the 1790s

Corsham's church of St Bartholomew

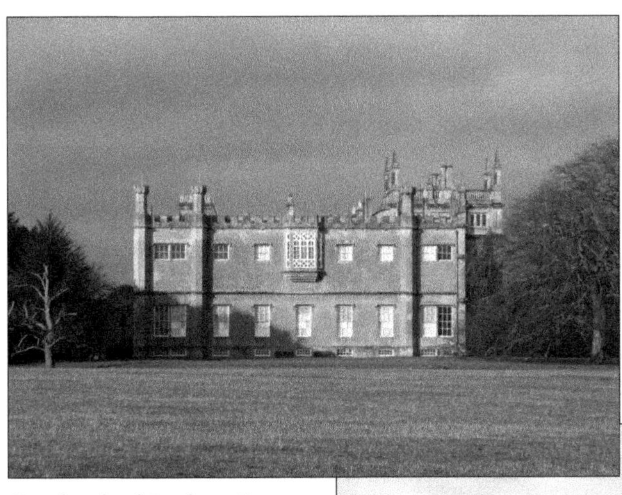

East façade of Corsham Court seen from the Park. It is the ground floor of this part of the building which houses the art collection open to the public

A section of the extensive ha ha in Corsham Park

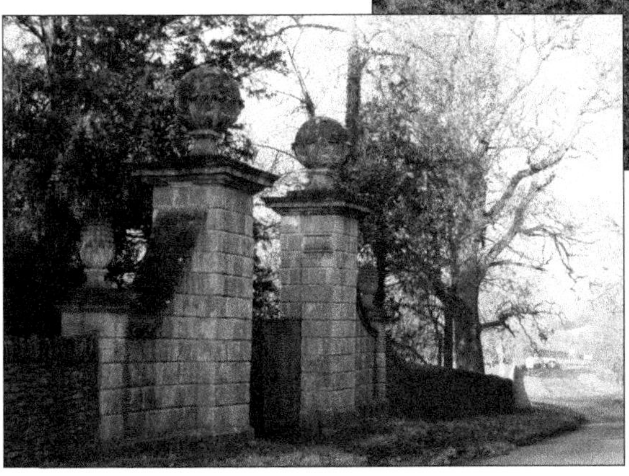

Grand entrance to former drive to Corsham Court

far side of the low stone wall away to your L. You will see the western outskirts of Chippenham ahead. Pass through another XG and finally exit Corsham Park by a gate at a junction with the main road.

Turn R here and follow this generally quiet lane past a grand **entrance gate** which formerly gave access to a drive through the wood to reach Corsham Court.

Pass a lane leading off to the R, then look out for an indicated PF sign and ST on your R. Two rights of way are possible from here. Take the one to the R which leads you, very slightly to the L, to a gap in the fence and again straight on to a stone slab ST, a few yards to the R of the buildings of Easton.

Cross the next field to reach a gate and ST in the far L corner. Cross the lane here and climb over the stone slab ST beside the PF sign, again to the R of buildings. Cross this field to reach a similar ST, just to the L of a cattle trough beside the stone wall opposite.

Now there is a change of direction. Bear R to find a double step ST, carrying a PF sign. Cross over and follow the boundary wall of **Rose and Unicorn House**, then bear L by a stony track. Bear L at the lane, continue past **Park Farm** and look out for an indicated PF on the R. Cross here and head diagonally L towards a wooden XG. Pass through and follow a fenced path.

Once you emerge into the open you will see the **spire** of St Bartholomew's and the façade of **Corsham Court** ahead. Closer to hand, on your R, is the watery expanse of **Corsham Lake**. Cross the ST beside a gate and carry on via the stony path to reach the XG into the churchyard.

*

Corsham has many treasures, not least the variety of its buildings easily accessed by walking the length of its High Street, much of which is pedestrianised so a pleasure to stroll along.

Another site not to be missed is the Hungerford Almshouses. These are reached by making for the southern end of the High Street and turning L at the Methuen Arms. The Hungerford Almshouses, which are open to the public, date from the seventeenth century and are possibly the grandest and best preserved of any almshouses in England.

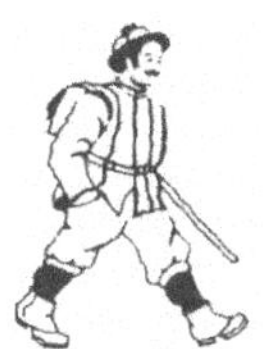

7 CORSHAM 2

via Biddestone and By Brook

Distance:	12 km. 7½ miles
Map:	Explorer 156
Map Reference:	705874
Refreshments en route:	The usual range of facilities in Corsham: the White Horse pub in Biddestone

THE WALK is very much a walk of two halves which together add up to one of the longer walks in this book. The first half, from Corsham to Biddestone, is mainly on the level along lanes and field paths. Corsham is a most attractive, pedestrian-friendly small town and Biddestone, within the Cotswold Area of Outstanding Natural Beauty, is a handsome village with, at its centre, manicured greens and a pond populated by ducks – all surrounded by fine houses. On leaving Biddestone we enter a less frequented country and descend to Weavern Lane following the well-wooded and steep-sided valley of the By Brook which here forms a section of the Macmillan Way. There is a short, sharp climb towards the end of the walk which returns to Corsham via Pickwick. Following a period of wet weather, the mostly unpaved Weavern Lane can by heavy going so that this walk is best reserved for a dry spell.

DIRECTIONS

Head north along pedestrianised **Corsham High Street**, past Post Office Lane, the Tourist Information Centre, Church Street and Priory Street, past the remarkably sculpted yew hedge which appears to be surging over the stone wall. At the junction, cross over and head along the road signposted **Bences Lane/The Laggar**. Pass the grandly named **Corsham Regis Primary**

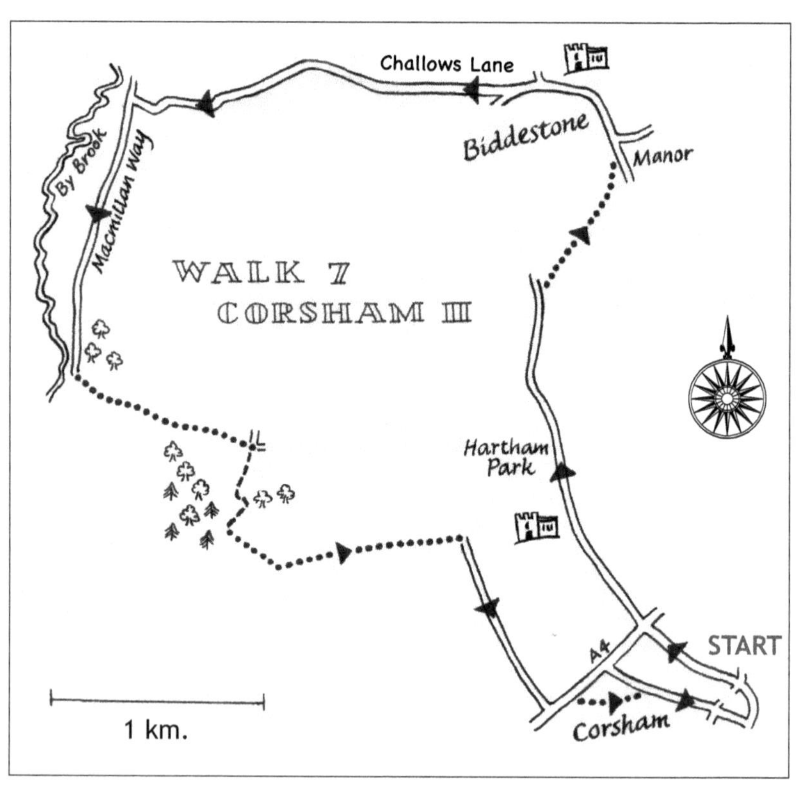

Challows Lane
By Brook
Macmillan Way
Biddestone
Manor
WALK 7
CORSHAM III
Hartham Park
A4
Corsham
START
1 km.

Academy (presumably the local school) and carry on to reach the main road, the A4.

Take care crossing to reach **Hartham Lane** opposite. The tower of Hartham Park Chapel soon comes into view ahead. It is reached by the Church Lodge and the forbidding notice 'Private Church Road' so no chance of visiting the church, the gate to which is generally kept locked anyway. Continue along the lane past the entrance gates to **Hartham Park**, seen to the L surmounted by a belfry, and the buildings of **Hartham Farm**.

Walk on past the farm and occasional dwellings lining the lane. On reaching Privet Cottage on the L, look out for a PF sign on your R beside a stone slab ST. Head across the field in a half-L direction to reach a metal gate, conspicuous in the hedgerow. There are two rights of way heading off from here. Make for the field gate to your R. In the next field head towards the far L corner and another metal gate.

On reaching a track, bear R and very soon L by a beaten path. Now head for a gate to enter a field. Continue towards a pair of gates to reach the next field. Now take a diagonal course towards the chimneys of Biddestone Manor to reach a field gate and original latch stile in the far R corner beside and the Corsham-Biddestone road.

Bear L, pass **Biddestone Manor** with its amusing topiary, the Biddestone Stud and, further along, the **White Hart** pub. Continue through the spacious and picturesque centre of the village with its wide green and duck pond. Bear L into **Church Road**.

> The village church of St Nicholas is surprisingly small for such an impressive seeming village but worth a visit with its neat box pews, gallery and memorials to countless Littles and Mountjoys.

Just beyond the church bear R along **Challows Lane** and carry on for about a mile. The views grow more interesting as you progress; a valley opens out to your L to merge with the one beyond. The lane begins to descend until it hits a **T-junction** and a way indicated **Weavern Lane**. Turn L. You have now joined a section of the Macmillan Way.

Continue along the lane and enjoy the views across the valley of the By Brook towards the wooded slopes opposite, though your view will be restricted when the trees are in leaf. Eventually the lane swings leftward,

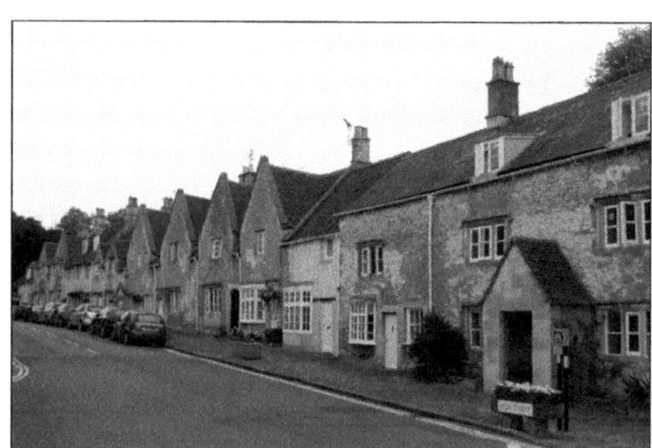

*Corsham
streetscapes*

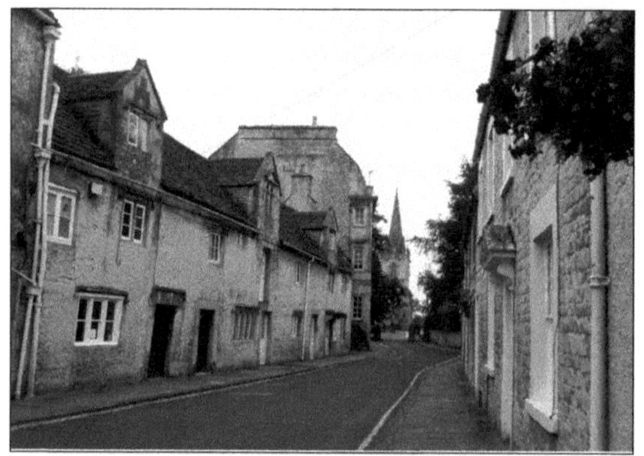

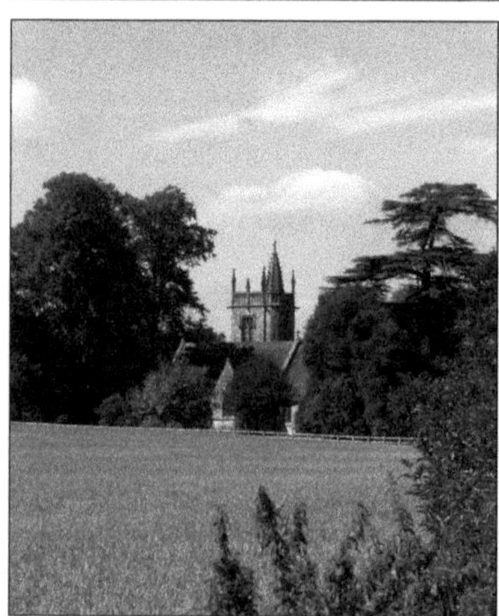

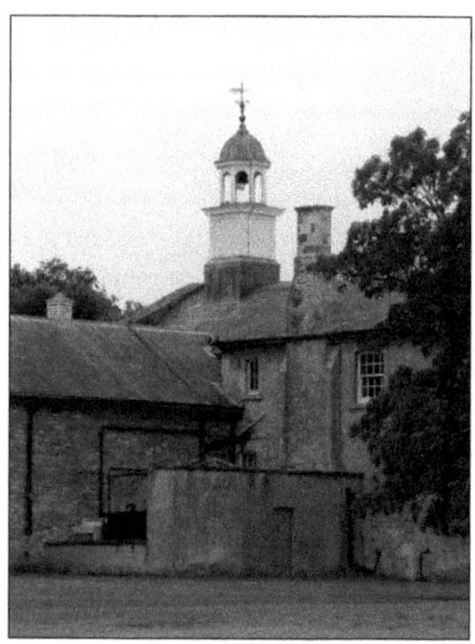

Harnham church across the fields; the belfry at Hartham Manor

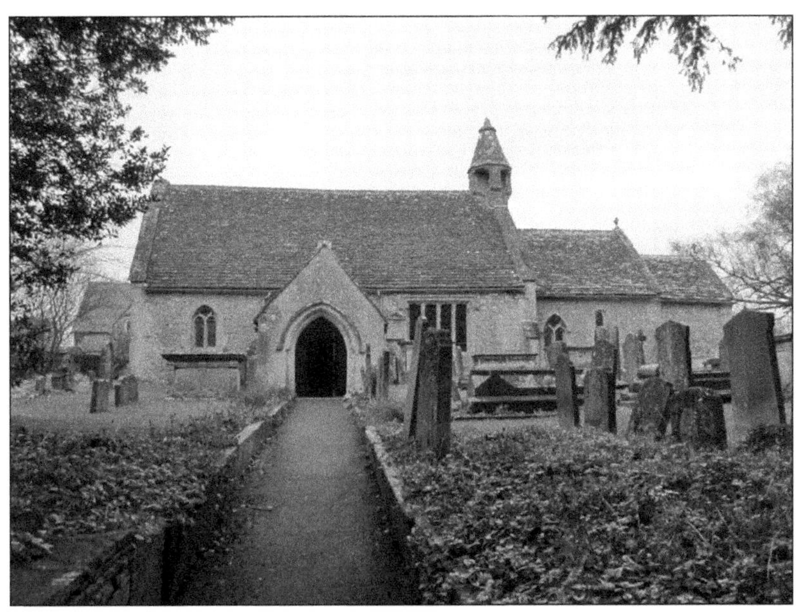

St Nicholas church, Biddestone

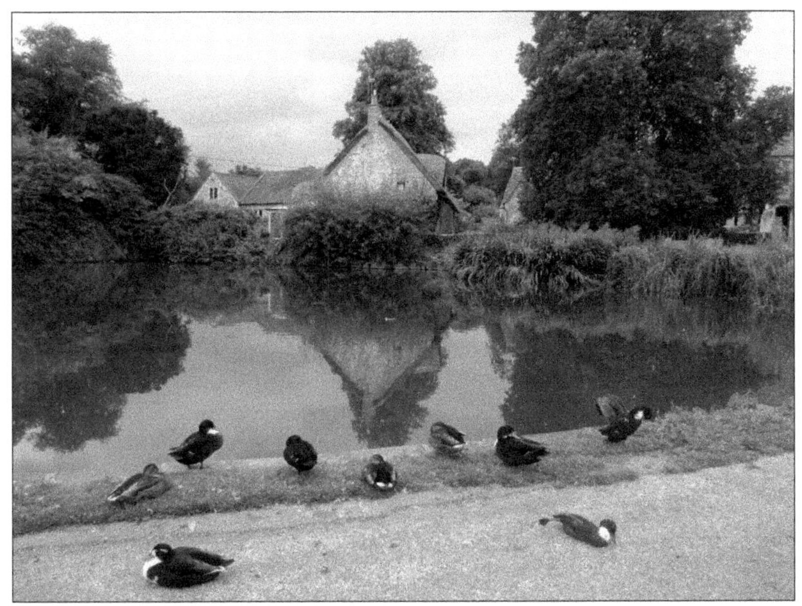

Biddestone village pond

becomes a hedged track and begins to climb. You pass a gate on your R which marks the continuation of the **Macmillan Way**. Look to your R here, in a south-westward direction, to take in the prospect along the valley of the By Brook as it continues its journey to join the Avon at Bathford. Note also the tower of Colerne Church on the skyline to the R.

Now continue to follow this lonely path until it levels out at a T-junction. Here you turn R along a wooded track which descends to reach a gate indicated Private. Bear L here along a signposted descending bridleway which becomes rather sunken and the natural habitat of ferns and mosses. Near the foot of this track you reach a signposted XG on the L.

Now you face a stiff climb – follow the beaten path to climb the steep hillside ahead. You eventually reach a metal XG. Go through and continue in the same direction to reach a PF sign beside a XG. Turn L here and head straight on beside the fence to your L. Continue in the same direction.

Another XG leads to a metalled drive and dwellings hereabouts. Walk straight ahead to reach the entrance to **Church Farm**, indicated as Private. Turn R here. This is **Middlewick Lane** – you may spot the tower of Hartham church away to your L – which you follow until you reach the main road, the **A4**, once again. The Hare and Hounds pub is a short distance to the right.

Cross the road carefully, and bear L past Lancefield Place. Look out for a pair of cottages on your R bearing the date stone 1739 – the cottage on the R has the Dickensian name **Pumblechook**. Just to the L of these cottages is the start of a narrow walled path. Head along here, then cross a road and continue along the path.

You eventually reach residential Priory Street where you carry on in the same direction, past the **Three Brewers** pub and Corsham Baptist Church to reach the road junction where you began the walk. Continue straight ahead to reach the **High Street**.

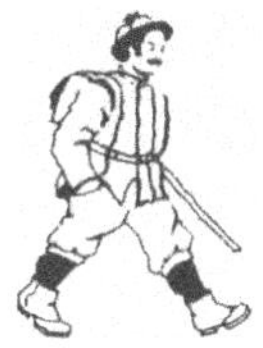

8 FAULKLAND

via Buckland Dinham, Hardington and Hemington

Distance:	10 km. 6¼ miles
Map:	Explorer 142
Map reference:	545739
Refreshments en route:	The Faulkland Inn pub; The Bell at Buckland Dinham

THE WALK is, inevitably, somewhat up and down. This is because both Faulkland and Buckland Dinham are ridge-top villages so that one must descend from and ascend to each one. The height involved is around 150 feet so it's never over-strenuous but there are some far-reaching views. Both are attractive villages though each lies on a fairly busy road, neither of which we have to cross. The hinterland between contains the settlements of Hemington – which boasts a school and impressive church – and Hardington, with its extensive farm buildings surrounding a small redundant church. This is a pleasant walk largely by field paths.

DIRECTIONS

Opposite Faulkland **village green** make for the PF sign and follow the path beside the pond. Once past the houses look out for a PF sign pointing L towards a ST beside a gate. Cross here and follow the hedgerow on your L.

Where the hedge ends, carry on, bearing slightly to the R to reach a XG in the hedge beyond. Once again follow the hedge on your L to reach a KG which leads you another field. Now follow the hedge to reach a lane.

Cross over and continue by the stony track opposite which begins a steady descent.

There is a wide view from hereabouts across the green patchwork of fields and hedgerows and towards the tower of **Buckland Dinham church** on the far ridge.

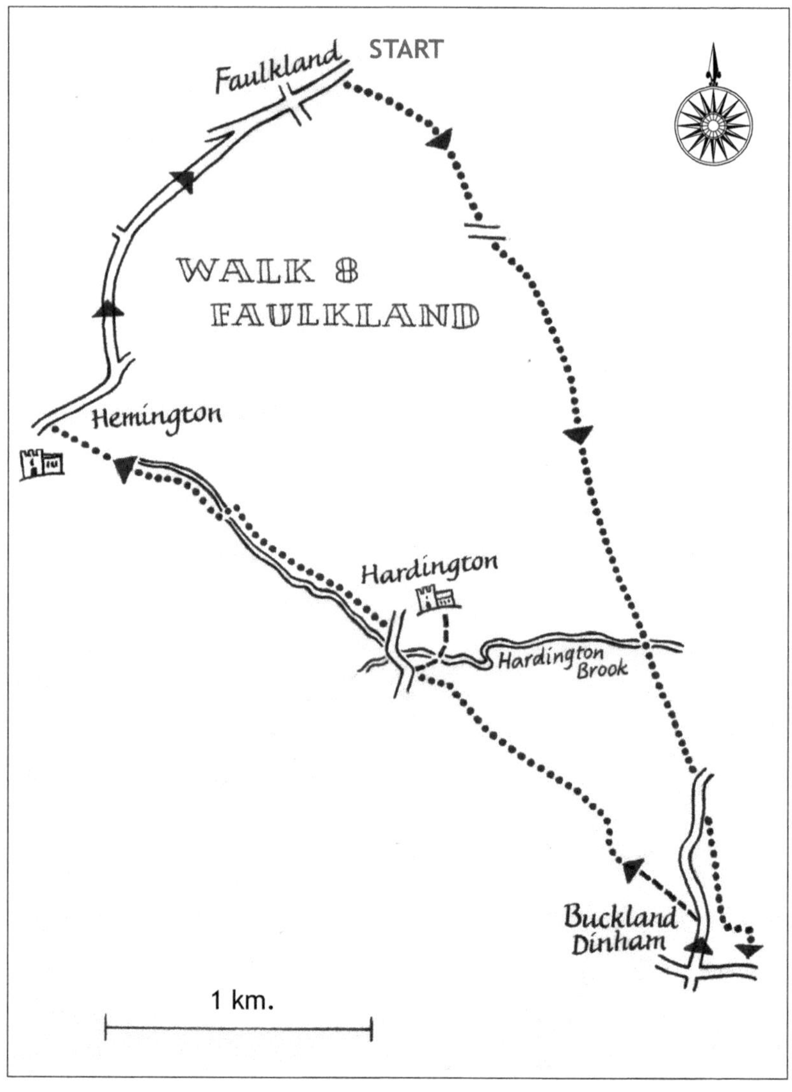

At the end of this track simply carry on with the hedgerow on your R. Look out for a ST about 100 metres to the L of the bottom corner of the field, then a second field. Follow the same direction to cross a couple more fields to cross a ST and footbridge to reach a track. Cross to a further ST opposite.

Go through here where there is a small rise ahead, from the summit of which you will see the church tower at Buckland Dinham drawing closer. Head to the R and follow the field boundary on your R, until you reach a gate in the hedgerow about a hundred metres before the foot of the field.

Now head in the same direction towards a gate in the wire fence ahead. Proceed across this low-lying and sometimes waterlogged field to reach a footbridge to cross **Hardington Brook**. If you have difficulty in locating the bridge simply plot a direct line from your last two field crossings.

> You may spot the buildings of **Hardington Farm** not far away to your R although it is usually difficult to pick out the pinnacles atop the tower of little St Mary's Church.

Carry straight on to pass through a farm gate and into a final field. Head to the R of the house to reach the lane which rises to meet the Bell pub in Buckland Dinham.

However, if you prefer to continue by an off-road route and see more of the village, cross the ST not far along on the L. Now climb the fairly steep slope to a XG at top L. The tower of Buckland Dinham church is straight ahead.

Turn R over a ST opposite a barn and follow the hedge on your L towards a final ST to reach the road through the village. The church will be found by turning L and L again, the Bell pub by turning R.

With your back to **The Bell**, turn R along the lane signposted to **Laverton and Wolverton**. Pass the Buckland Bell camp site and peel off by the track to the L (not the one indicated to the R), gradually descending. Pas through the the gate at the foot of the incline and bear R to follow the hedgerow for a few hundred metres and reach a ST. Cross here and carry on with the hedgerow to your R and a row of trees on ascending ground to your L. Cross into the following field, in the same direction, again for some distance, to reach a gate closely followed by another, to reach a concrete track.

Turn R here if you wish to view the redundant church of St Mary. You will find it completely surrounded by the buildings of Manor Farm. To resume the walk there is no right of way through the farm so you must retrace your steps.

If you have not diverted to visit Hardington church, bear L along the concrete track and R when you reach the lane. Cross the Brook and look out for a Public Bridleway sign indicating a route to the L. You will very soon reach a KG on the R. Go through this and follow the brook to your L in the same north-westerly direction you have followed since leaving Buckland Dinham.

Pass into a second field at the end of which you head L to cross the brook. Pass thrugh a gate and follow an enclosed path. This in turn leads on to a meandering path through a wood, across a stream once more, then into a tapering field and once again to an enclosed path towards the lane through **Hemington**.

You will spot the tower of Hemington church to the L. Our route is to the R but, if you wish to visit the church, bear L.

Back on track we pass the village school, Hemington First School, then a former Primitive Methodist Chapel (1869), and finally past a neat row of dwellings bearing the inscription Jubilee Cottages, 1887. Beyond these, take the L fork to climb **Tyning Hill**.

Fork R at the summit. This quiet lane will lead you directly to Faulkland where you bear R along the pavement beside the main road to reach your starting point.

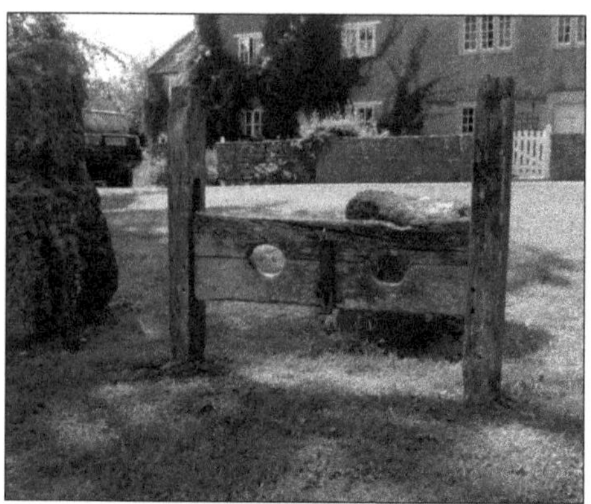
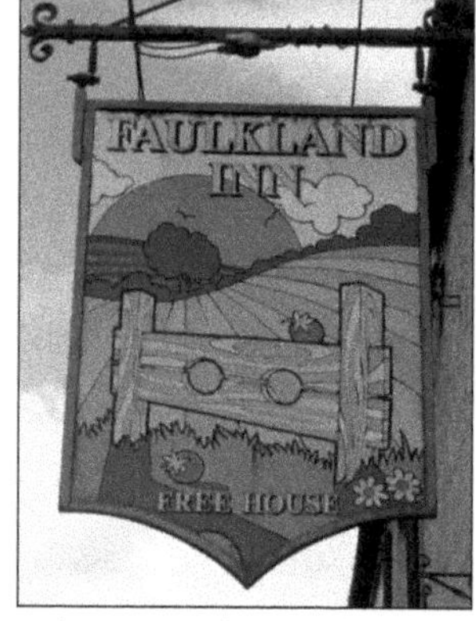

Stocks on Faulkland village green and as depicted on the sign at the Faulkland Inn

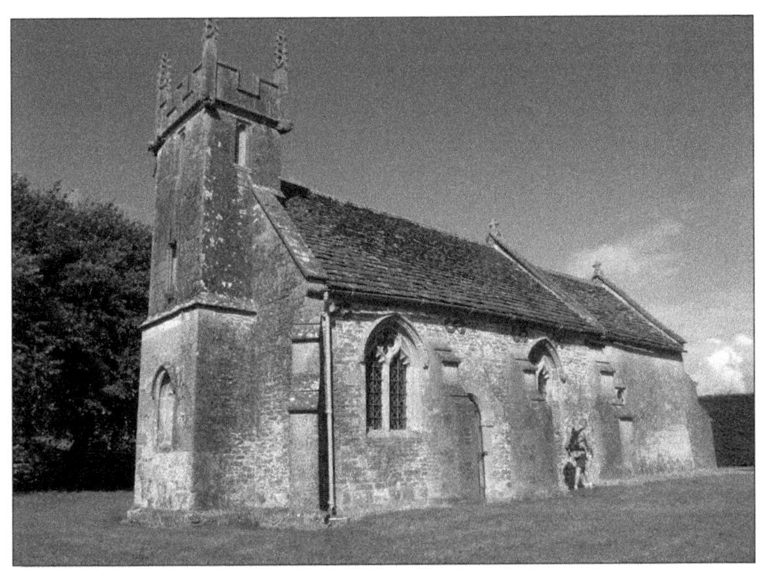

The little redundant church of St Mary, Hardington

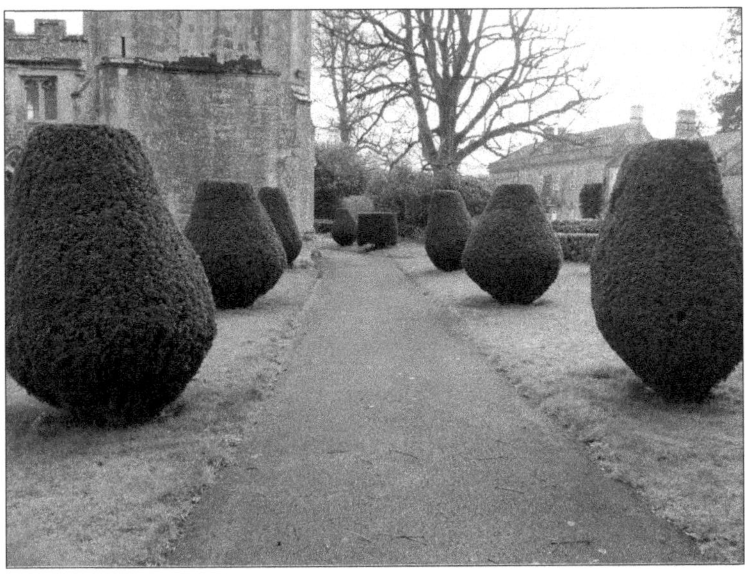

*Clipped yews standing to attention beside the path to Hemington Church,
also dedicated to St Mary*

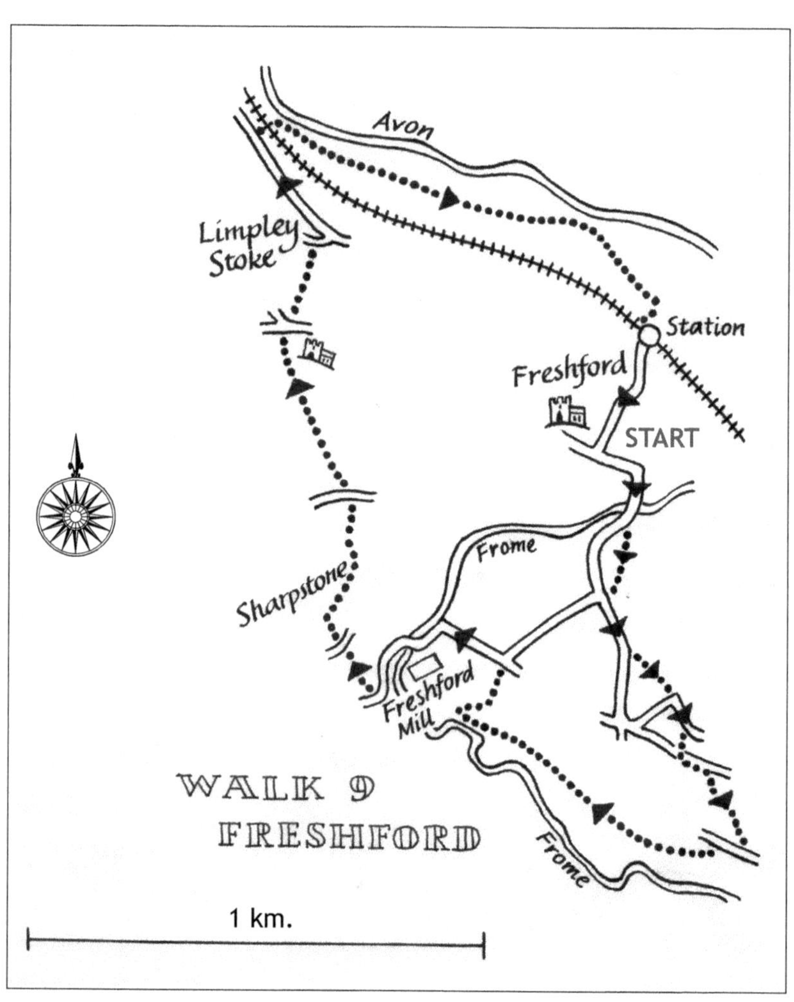

Avon
Limpley
Stoke
Station
Freshford
START
Frome
Sharpstone
Freshford
Mill
Frome
WALK 9
FRESHFORD
1 km.

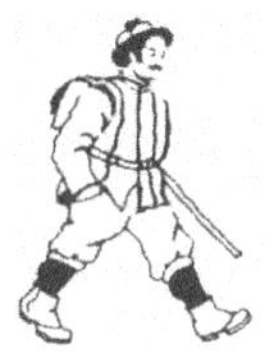

9 FRESHFORD

via Limpley Stoke

Distance:	5½ km. 3½ miles
Map:	Explorers 143 and 155
Map reference:	603784
Refreshments en route:	The Galleries Café at Freshford (at about half-way); The Inn at Freshford soon after the start; The Hope Pole in Limpley Stoke is a short distance from the route.

THE WALK is extremely varied but, it must be said, fairly demanding with many ascents and descents, sometimes by steps where care is required. Freshford is a hilly village so its many interesting and attractive buildings are well scattered about its slopes and valleys; it also possesses a remarkable network of footpaths. The route follows lanes and paths beside both the Rivers Frome and Avon and all but describes a figure of eight so that the walk may be undertaken in two halves.

DIRECTIONS

Parking is generally to be had along the road near The Inn and bridge across the river Frome. Cross the bridge from the pub side and look out for the PF sign and XG located a few yards further along. Enter the field here and follow the beaten path with the hedgerow on your R, then exit the field to rejoin the road.

Bear L, uphill, towards the tall terrace of houses. Look for the PF on your L immediately past the house named **Thurleigh**. Follow this narrow path uphill until it delivers you back at the road.

Cross over and head further uphill to reach the path on the R beside the **post box**. Now descend the steps until you reach a way to your L past a row of cottages with views across the valley to your R.

Just past the last dwelling, No 9: Halfway House, bear R to follow a narrow footpath downhill beside a garden boundary. Lower down you are directed to the L to enter a wood. Follow the roughly beaten way which soon meets the lane below.

Cross directly to the stone slab ST and wooden gate opposite. Enter the field here and bear R with the river to your L and, further along, the scattered dwellings of Friary on the far bank. Continue heading down-river until the field narrows at a point where the waters of the River Frome drive a water turbine. You now ascend a short distance to reach an open field.

To your L is the development at **Freshford Mill** which has been under construction for many years.

Cross the field to reach the lane by a XG. The lane ahead leads to the bridge across the Frome which you crossed earlier. If you wish, you could end the walk here and return to Freshford.

But, to continue, bear L towards the mill and bridge. Cross over, bear L and soon reach a minor junction. Look for the PF to the R. Go through the XG and climb the steps uphill. Cross a lane and continue by the steps opposite.

This steep climb will take you to a XG facing an open field. Bear R beside the hedgerow to enjoy some great views up the Limpley Stoke Valley, across to Staples Hill and, in the distance to the R, as far as Westbury White Horse.

Exit this field by a XG in the R-hand corner, take the L fork in the path then R to follow the path downhill beside gardens until you reach the lane with **The Galleries Community Shop and Café** opposite.

The way now is straight on beside the shop to your R and **Village Hall** to your L. Head through the playground and beyond through a XG. You will spot the diminutive tower and spire of **Limpley Stoke church** on the hilltop as you ascend to it.

You reach the an information board beside Limpley Stoke church. Cross the road and carry on by the PF opposite. This takes you downhill and across a lane to reach the road through Lower Stoke. Turn L here to descend **Crowe Hill**. At a low point look out for a PF leading to the R and indicating Freshford 1½ miles. Pass beneath the railway and bear R with the River Avon away to your left and Upper Westwood on the skyline ahead. Cross a ST and keep walking until the track heads to the R towards the footbridge at **Freshford Station**. Cross the footbridge and head along **Station Road** to reach **The Hill** in **Freshford**. Bear L for The Inn and your starting point.

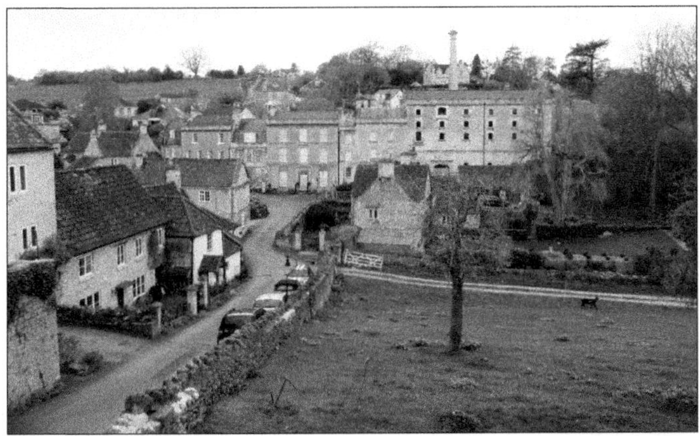

View from Freshford churchyard

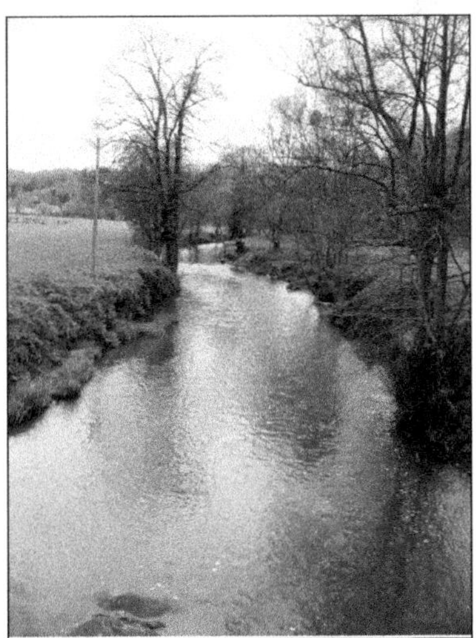

River Frome from Freshford Bridge

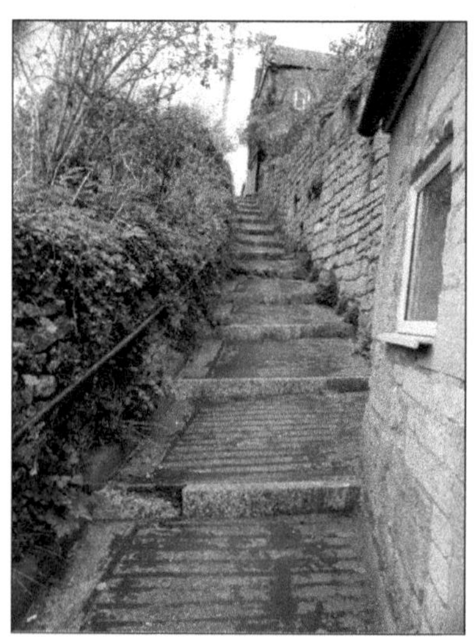

*Stone steps linking cottages
to Staples Hill*

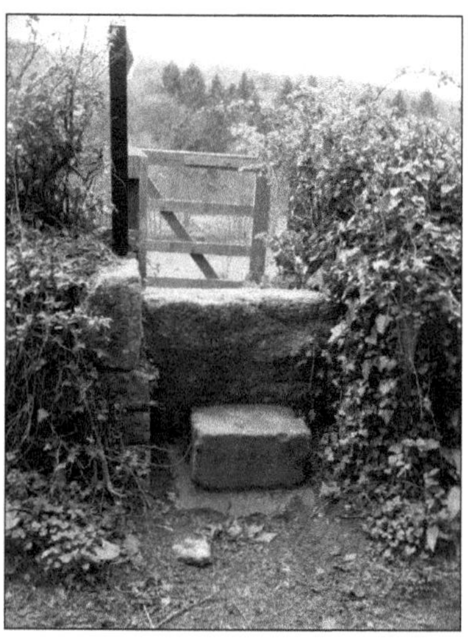

Stone stile beside Iford Lane

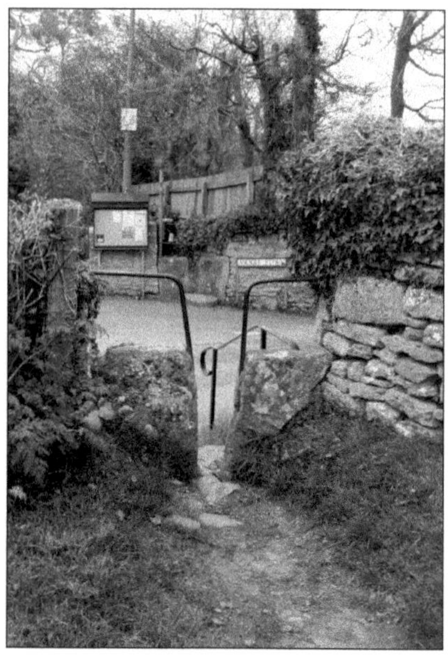

*Approaching Middle Stoke
beside Limpley Stoke church*

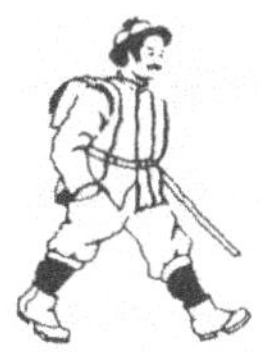

10 HEYTESBURY

via Corton and Upton Lovell

Distance:	9.5 km. 6 miles
Map:	Explorer 143
Map reference:	426925
Refreshments en route:	A shop and two pubs, the Red Lion and The Angel, in Heytesbury; the Dove Inn at Corton and the Prince Leopold at Upton Lovell.

THE WALK is mostly on the level with the exception of one steady climb through some 150 feet up a Bridleway from Corton. Heytesbury is an interesting village which for many years has been happily bypassed by the A36. The route crosses the Wylye valley to Corton, climbs the edge of the downs to give a superb view, then back again via the smaller communities of Upton Lovell and Knook with one or two surprises en route.

DIRECTIONS

In **Heytesbury Main Street** locate the Red Lion pub, beside which is the village shop and Post Office. Head past the shop towards the **church of St Peter and St Paul** and through the churchyard towards the far side where you join **Mill Street.**

Look out for the PF sign pointing along **Mantles Lane** beside the **River Wylye**, a typically clear and swiftly flowing chalk stream. Here you are following a section of the Wessex Ridgeway. Carry on towards the mill buildings ahead, then bear L as you approach the weir and R to reach a XG to join the lane where you turn R.

Cross the river and bear immediatey L by the path signposted as the **Wessex Ridgeway.** Cross a couple of wooden footbridges to emerge at

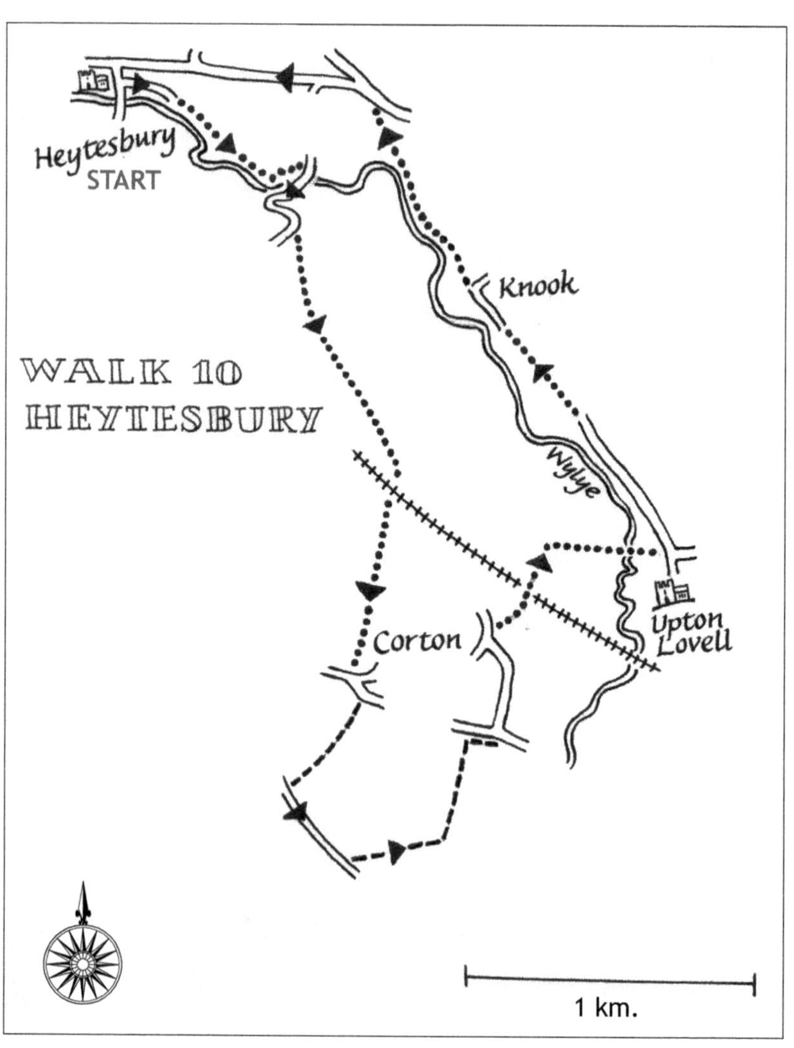

Heytesbury
START
WALK 10
HEYTESBURY
Knook
Wylye
Corton
Upton
Lovell
1 km.

a lane. Our route heads along a farm track immediately to the L, as indicated by a PF sign opposite. Follow this straight ahead for some distance until you reach a tunnel beneath the embanked railway track.

Once through here and the XG on the far side turn R to follow the hedgerow first to your R, then to your L and straight on to reach the road and the hamlet of **Corton.** Turn L at the road. At the fork you will spot the attractive building of the **Dove Inn** away to your L.

Keep to the R here, still on the main road and look out for the Bridleway heading uphill just to the R of **Foley's Cottage.** Here you are back on a stretch of the Wessex Ridgeway. Head up this hedged track, rising steadily. Ignore the drive on the L marked Private Road but carry on a few more yards to reach a small junction.

Turn L, follow the lane and enjoy the view across the Wylye Valley from this vantage point, some 150 feet above Corton. You are looking towards Knook Hill with the ever-busy A36 traversing its lower slope.

After 200 metres or so, look for a **farm gate** on your L. Just inside the field is a sign indicating **Restricted Byway**. Enter the field and cross over again immediately to your L. Now follow the hedgerow on your R for a short distance before forsaking it to descend in the same general direction towards the gate below (not the sharp descent to the L).

Now go through two gates, then a wooden stile on your L (not the one straight ahead) to follow a track. On reaching an exit to the lane continue by the track as it turns R to follow the hedgerow to reach a gate where you leave the field.

Now head straight ahead by the lane opposite indicated as 'Unsuitable for Heavy Goods Vehicles'. When you reach the entrance gates to Corton House look out for a signposted PF on your R. Head along here, beside a stream, then across the **railway line**, taking heed to STOP, LOOK and LISTEN.

Follow the hedged path to a junction of field boundaries, marked by a XG. Here you bear R and cross the Wylye to reach **Upton Lovell.**

Possible short detour: If you wish to visit the village church you can do so by turning R at the minor junction and walking a short distance.

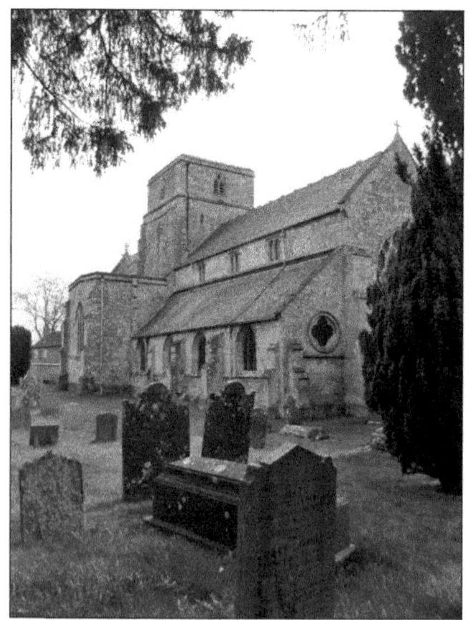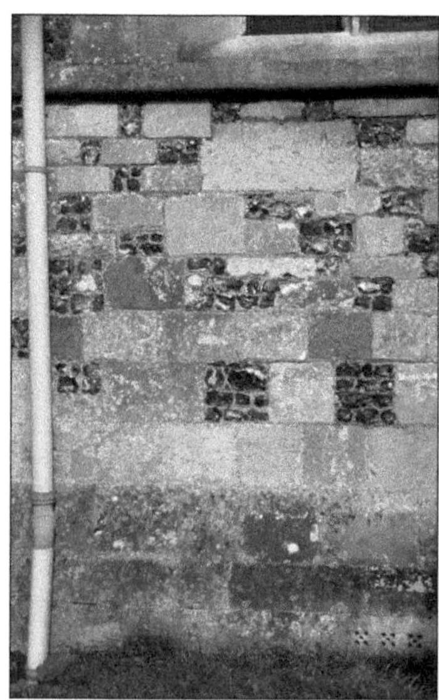

The church of St Peter and St Paul, Heytesbury; its chequerboard walls

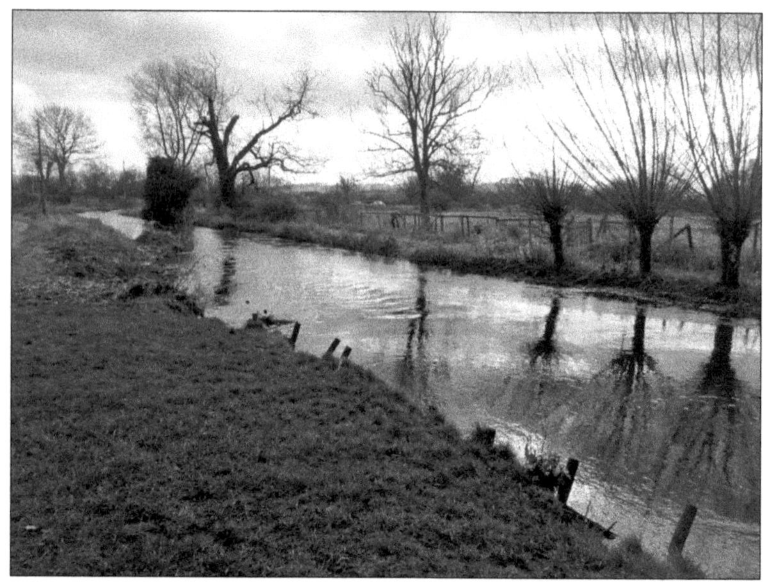

The River Wylye, tributary of the Salisbury Avon, connects Heytesbury,
Knook and Upton Lovell

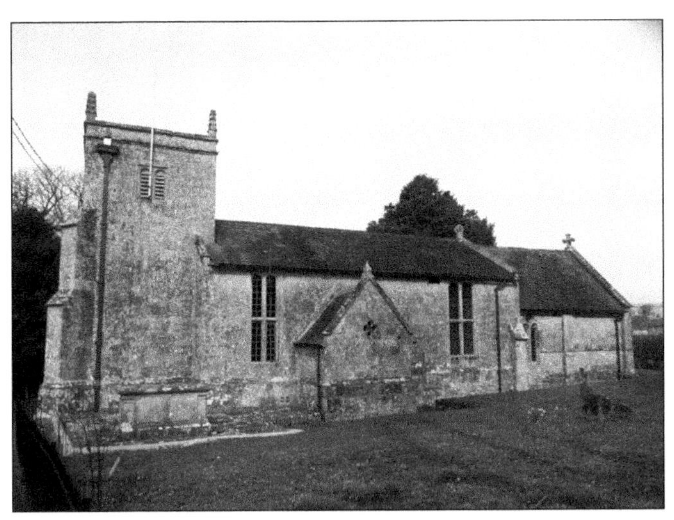

The little church of St Augustine, Upton Lovell

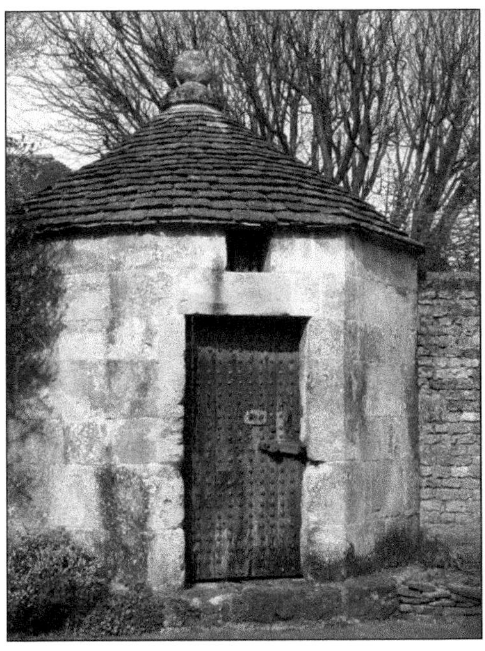

The blind house beside the road in Heytesbury

To continue the walk turn L here. You will shortly reach the **Prince Leopold**, the Inn on the River, which has an attractive outside area overlooking the River Wylye. Carry straight on; at No 69 the lane reverts to a footpath, then a fieldpath beside a hedge. Head straight on beside **East Farm** to reach a minor crossroads.

This is the hamlet of **Knook**. Here, to your L, you will spot the ancient church dedicated to St Margaret of Antioch.

Once again, continue by a track in the same direction. You will catch glimpses ot the swiftly flowing Wylie on your L. You may be interested to pass the Birdhenge sculpture garden on your R.

The sound of the A36 grows closer but, mercifully, you are saved from direct contact. The path merges with the old road which once carried the A36 through Heytesbury main street before the village was bypassed in the 1980s. As you head back to the starting point you will pass The Angel Inn, plus the impressive **Hungerford Almshouses**. Look out, too, for the neat little blind house.

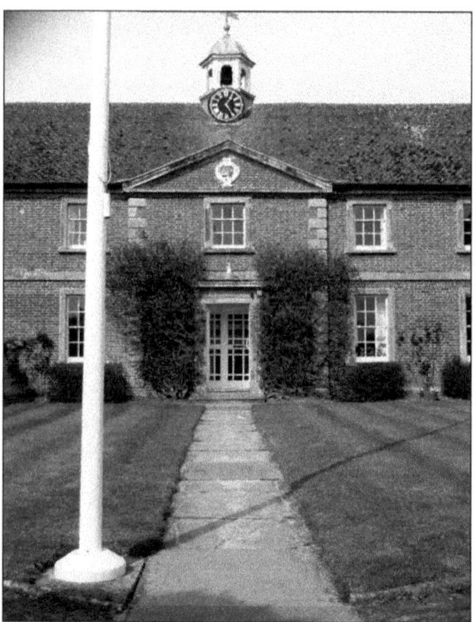

The Hospital of St John, Heytesbury. This fine Georgian building dates from 1769, though the foundation dates back to 1449

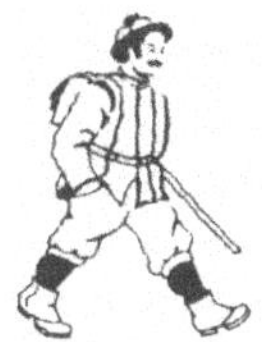

11 KILMERSDON

via Vobster

Distance:	9¼ km. 6 miles
Map:	Explorer 142
Map reference:	524696
Refreshments en route:	The Jolliffe Arms in Kilmersdon

THE WALK requires a steepish ascent through a wood to reach Babington House after which the route is fairly level or undulating. No other village is visited on the course of the walk but highlights include Babington House and church, a view down to the flooded former quarry at Vobster (though this may be all but obscured in summer) and a very pleasant final mile along a minor valley, the first half of which is beside a stream.

DIRECTIONS

To begin the walk from the centre of **Kilmersdon**: with your back to the **Jolliffe Arms**, bear L along the **main street**. As the road veers to the L you will pass **The Thatched Cottage** on your R, at the entrance to **Hoare's Lane**. A short way further is a PF sign beside a XG. Cross here and follow the hedgerow on your L.

Cross into a second field and follow the beaten path ahead to cross a ST. This way veers to the R as you approach the woods and stream ahead.

Carry on along a field edge to reach a footbridge. Cross over and begin to ascend a slope through the woods by a clearly defined path. You eventually emerge into a level field by a pair of **grand gate posts**. Cross the field towards a XG to walk by a pond on your R. Carry on until you spot impressive **Babington House** and, backing on to the path, the Georgian gem of St Margaret's Church.

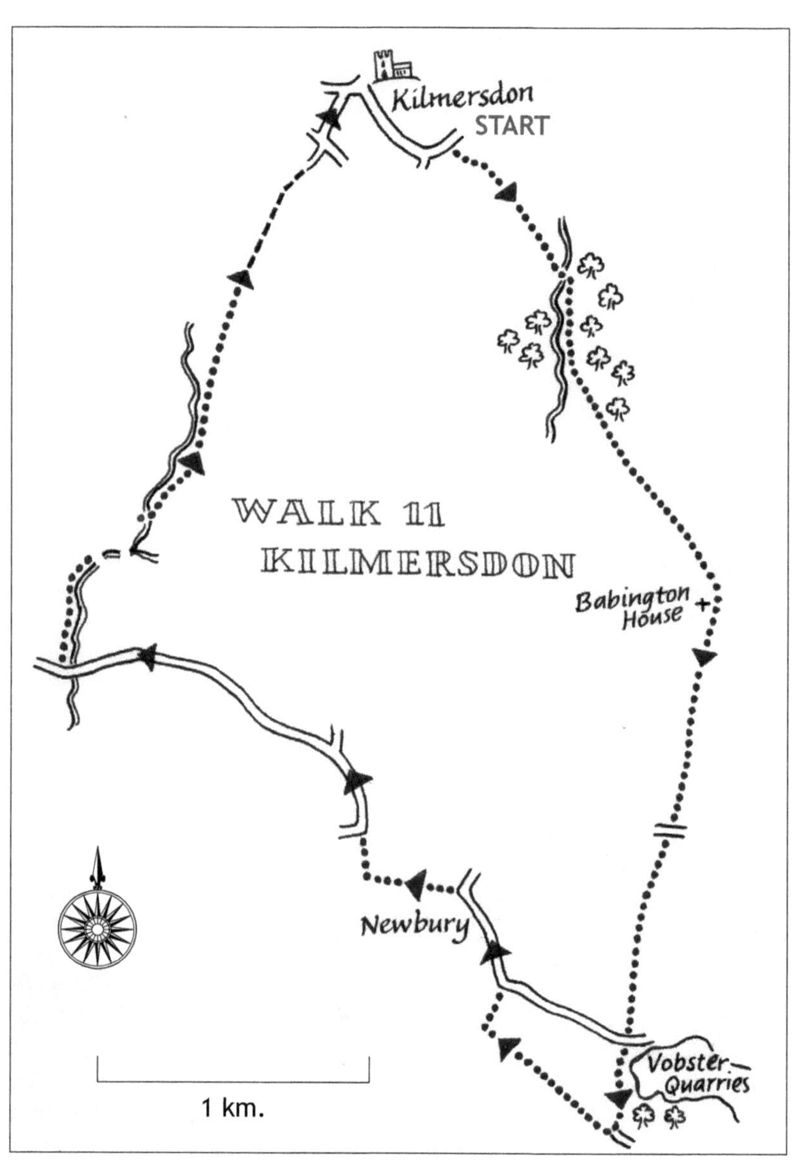

Kilmersdon
START
WALK 11
KILMERSDON
Babington
House
Newbury
Vobster
Quarries
1 km.

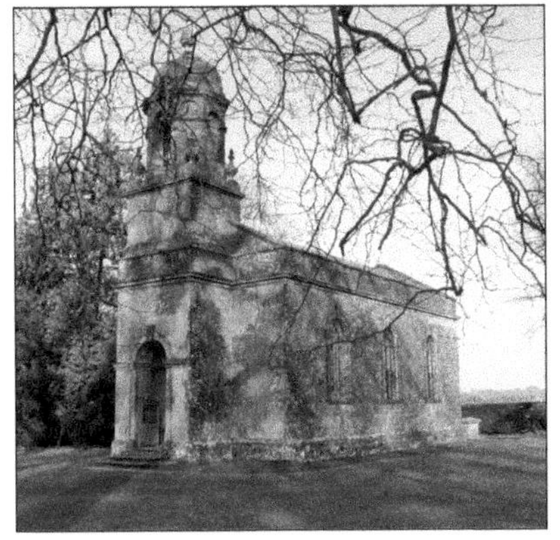

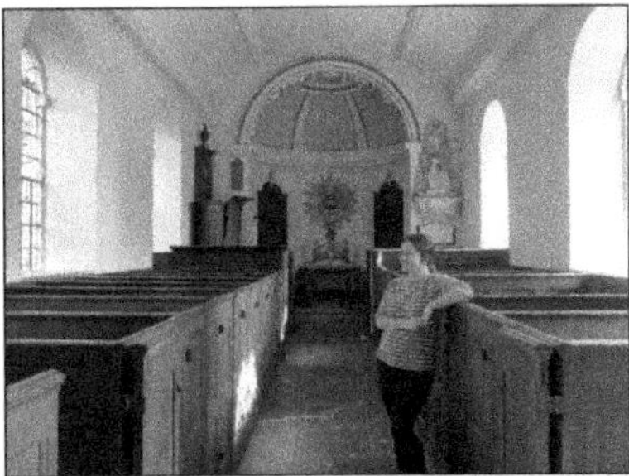

*The tiny Georgian church in Babington
dedicated to St Margaret*

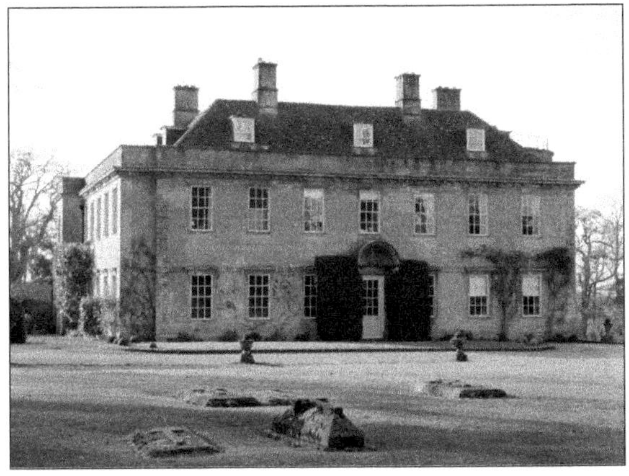

Babington House

Cross the drive and continue in the same direction by a signposted grassy and tree-lined path. You cross a lane beside a house to enter the field opposite. Carry on, a little to the right, to reach a field corner opposite. You will see two STs in the hedgerow ahead and to your right – cross the nearest one. Now bear L and follow the field boundary on your L to exit by a ST near the far L corner. Cross into the field directly opposite and gradually descend.

To your L, through the wire fence, you can look across a former quarry which is now flooded and home to the Vobster Diving School, an unexpected prospect from the edge of your green field.

Follow the fence to your left and drop down beside a house. Cross the drive to a ST ahead. Don't cross here but turn R along the track. Looking south across the valley below you can see the buildings lining the road through the ridge-top village of Highbury.

Once past the last house on your R, opposite the low building to the L, look out for a PF and XG on your R. Cross here and bear L, first between fences and then to the R towards a Bristol gate at the top L corner. Once through here bear R beside the hedgerow to exit by a ST and meet the lane. Now head on in the same direction.

Shortly past the houses to your L – the last one being a bungalow named **The Leos** – the lane bends to the right. Here look out for a pair of PF signs at a field opening on the L. Head straight across the field to reach a ST in the hedgerow on the far side.

In the following field bear R to reach the lane, then head straight on – not L. Very soon another lane joins from the R and then the way forks. Take the L fork (the R fork is Hoare's Lane which leads directly back to Kilmersdon).

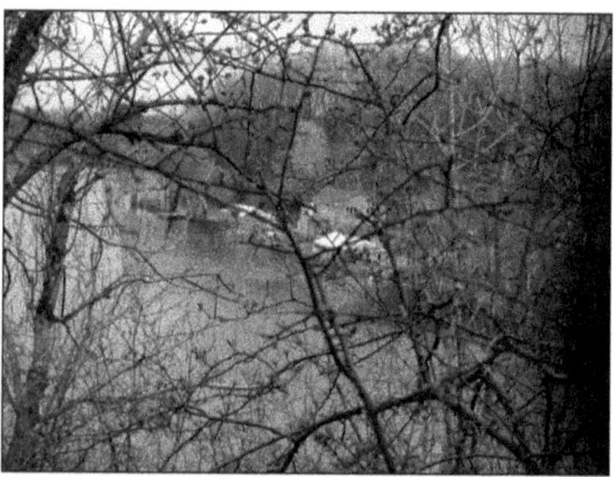

The flooded former Vobster quarry, now home of the Vobster Diving School, which at least proves there is a place name which rhymes with lobster.

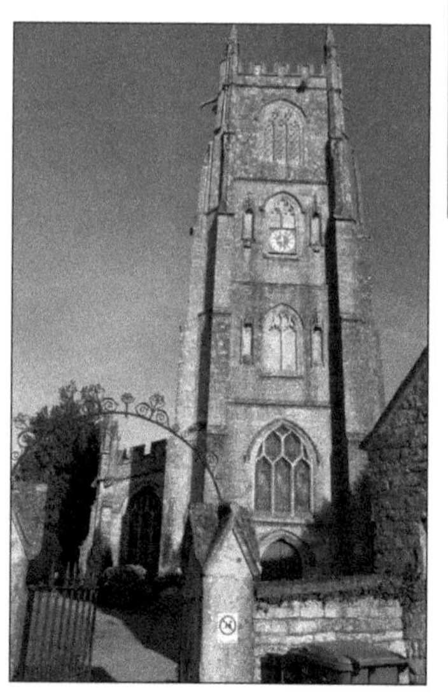

The imposing tower of St Peter and St Paul church in Kilmersdon, a former pit village whose colliery closed in 1973, the last one to close in the Somerset Coalfield

Follow the lane for some distance past **Luckington Stables** and **Cherry Garden Farm**. Begin to descend and look out for a signposted bridleway on the R. Enter the field here and immediately bear L to follow the hedgerow as it descends. Once in the dip at a point opposite Owls Nest Farm bear R and follow the path downstream.

You are soon joined by a second, larger stream, from the L. Cross to the opposite bank, but soon recross to the L by a bridge.

Pass through a gate and continue with the stream to your R. When the field narrows and tapers to a point you cross the stream once again. Head for a gate and simply follow the path beyond which eventually forsakes the stream that flows below to your L. You reach former farm buildings where the right of way is indicated straight ahead by a metalled track which leads you directly to the centre of Kilmersdon opposite the church tower.

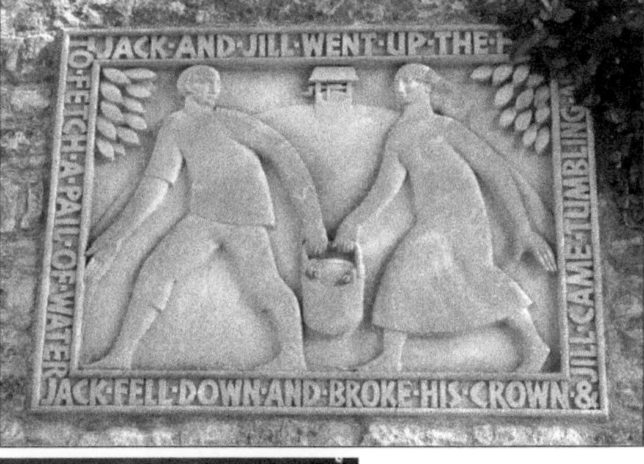

It is said that, centuries ago, Jack and Jill daily went up the hill for water. One fateful day Jack was hit by a boulder from nearby Badstone Quarry. He tumbled down and suffered a wound that not even vinegar and brown paper could mend. Jill also died young, but not before she had given birth to the couple's son whom villagers raised and called Jill's son. The surname Gilson still features widely in this area.

ERECTED: IN CELEBRATION OF THE YEAR 2000

No visit to Kilmersdon would be complete without following in the footsteps of Jack and Jill!

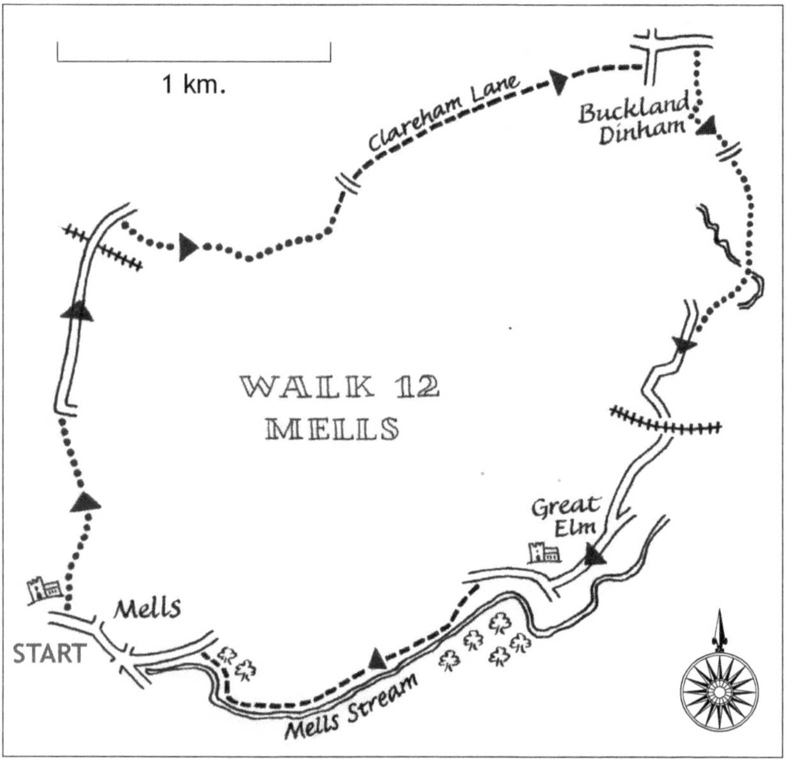

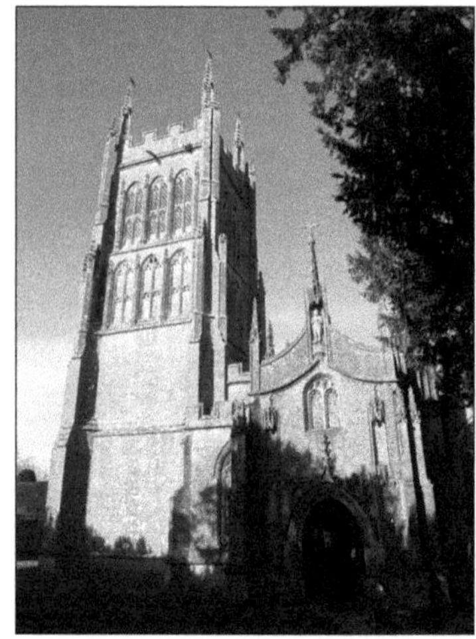
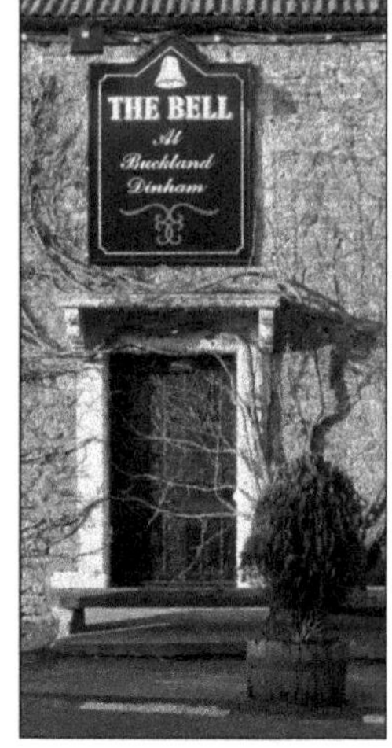

The soaring pinnacles of St Andrew's church in Mells; the Bell pub in Buckland Dinham

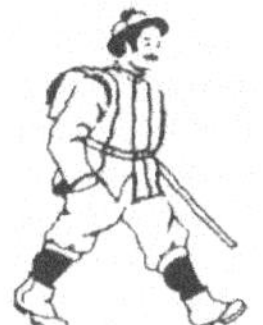

12 MELLS

via Buckland Dinham, Great Elm and Wadbury Valley

Distance:	9.5 km. 6 miles
Map:	Explorer 142
Map reference:	727493
Refreshments en route:	Mells: The Talbot Inn; shop and café
	Buckland Dinham: The Bell pub

THE WALK is by an attractive mix of field path, riverside path, hedged track and country lane centred on the exceptional village of Mells. Buckland Dinham with its friendly pub is the convenient half-way point. There is much to intrigue en route: the solitary but perfectly preserved brick chimney stack stranded in a field beside Clareham Lane on the way to Buckland, the mysterious notice beneath the railway arch towards Great Elm and, on the last leg back to Mells, the extensive ruins of Fussell's Edge Tool Works and impossible-seeming waterfall in the mini-gorge of Wadbury Valley.

DIRECTIONS

You will find the interesting **St Andrew's church** in the attractive stone-built village of Mells at the end of town-like New Street. Siegfried Sassoon and Violet Bonham-Carter, amongst other luminaries, are buried in its grounds and there is much of interest within.

At the far side of the church there is an avenue of yew trees which leads to an exit from the churchyard towards a rising slope.

Follow the beaten path and make the gentle ascent to reach a ST, a little to the R, in the hedge above. Cross the next field towards a gap in the hedge beyond, then head diagonally to the L to exit a third field by a ST in the far L corner. Now follow the lane ahead. You cross a former railway track which plays host to **Colliers Way,** a well signposted route for pedestrians and cyclists and part of the National Cycle Network.

Continue for around 200 metres and look carefully for an easily missed PF sign on your R. Descend to enter the field – and watch out for a ditch just before you reach it, then bear L to follow a lightly beaten path along a fairly even contour.

> This elevated path offers views far and wide, including across to the 100+ feet church tower in Mells to your R, the slender spire of Whatley church on the horizon to the L and the notched outline of Cley Hill.

Carry on to cross a track via a pair of STs. Do not make a direct descent but follow the line of trees to your R. This leads to a ST where you bear a little to the L to reach a track. You follow this for around a mile, past a minor junction at Hill House Farm, towards Buckland Dinham.

> This hedged track is named on the OS Explorer map as Clareham Lane. En route you will enjoy views towards Cley Hill and Westbury White Horse. You will also notice a mysterious tall, square-built, brick chimney rising from the field on your R. Consulting the OS map reveals this to be the remains of a coal mine. We know that the Somerset Coalfield lies not far away in the environs of Radstock and Midsomer Norton but this particular location would appear to be rather remote from it.

You reach the buildings of **Buckland Dinham** at a cross track. If you turn L here you will reach **The Bell** pub just across the main road through the village. Turn R along the street through the village (L if you're emerging from the pub). Further down, up a L turn, lies St John the Baptist church.

However, to continue the walk, make for the track opposite the **Old Post Office** and beside **Hill House**. Head up here to reach a ST.

Alternatively, and for a more direct route, avoid the main road but cross the ST opposite the end of Clareham Lane and head along the path at the backs of houses to reach a ST.

Cross over and carry on to cross a stone slab ST. Follow the hedge on your L. Another ST close to the L corner takes you into a field in which you follow the beaten path to descend to a ST onto a lane. Cross a stone ST opposite, then a metal gate. Buckland Brook flows to your L. Cross a footbridge.

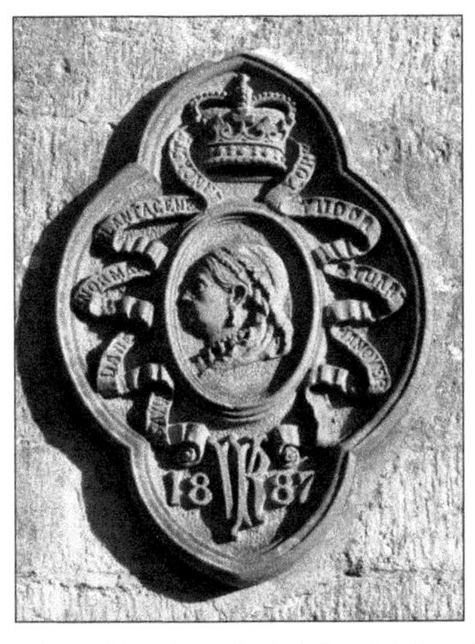

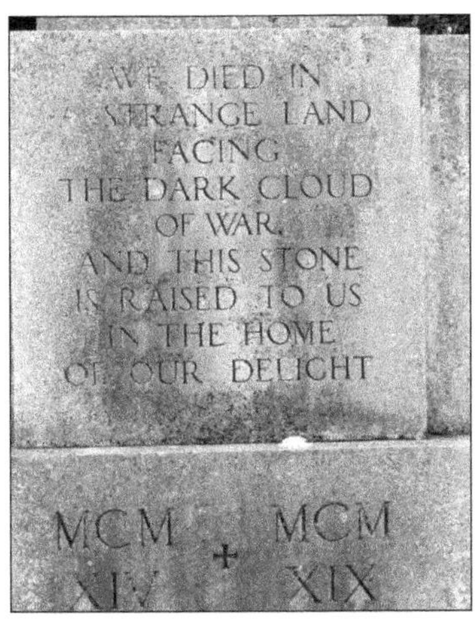

Above left: Victoria Golden Jubilee plaque in Mells listing Royal houses: Saxon, Dane, Norman, Plantagenet, Tudor, Stuart, Hanover

Above right: The poignant inscription commemorating the death of 20 men of Mells in the Great War: 'We have died in a strange land and facing the dark cloud of war, and this stone is raised to us in the home of our delight.'

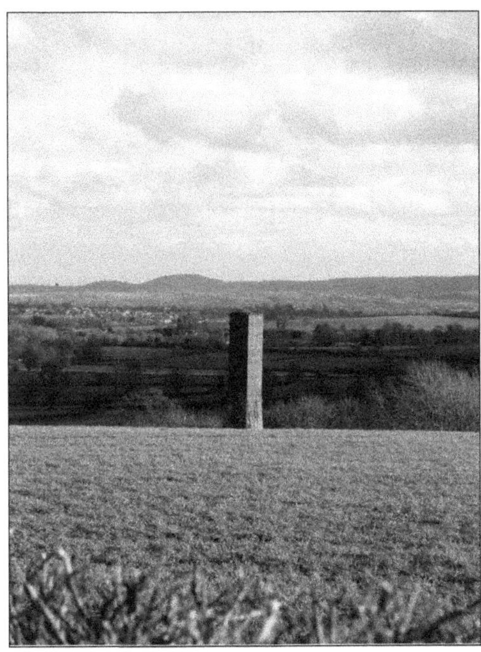

The solitary but well preserved brick chimney standing isolated in a field beside Clareham Lane en route to Buckland Dinham. The Explorer map indicates this as 'Chy' and 'Colliery (dis)' referring to the chimney of a disused colliery. Down and Warrington's book, The History of the Somerset Coalfield, omits any mention of this particular colliery but elsewhere I discovered that the Buckland Coal Syndicate bored a shaft here to a depth of 896 feet but that the enterprise failed due to continuous flooding below ground – presumably the engine which this chimney served was unable to cope.
Cley Hill in distance.

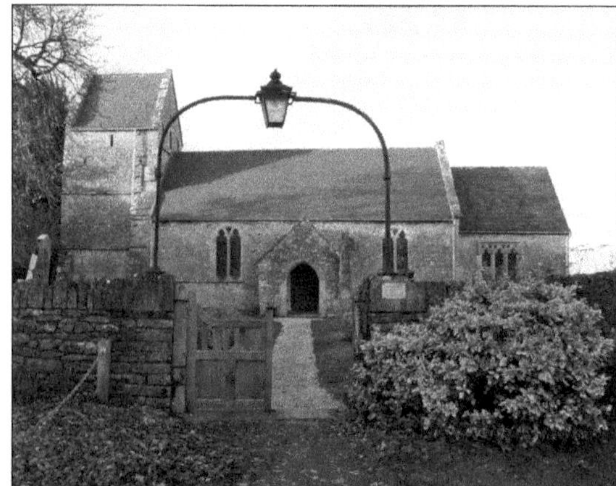

St Mary Magdalene, Great Elm, is quite an ancient church. Its interior is rather plain but fitted out with neat boxed pews. Walk around the churchyard to the rear of the church for a fine view cross country towards the tower of Buckland Dinham Church

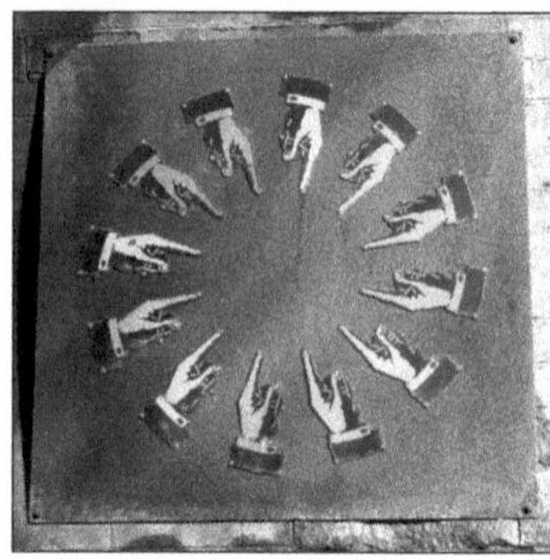

Mysterious sign, featuring 12 inward pointing manicules, affixed to roof of railway arch en route to Great Elm – one of a number of artworks which accompany the former railway line, now restored as a Sustrans cycle route

Moss and ferns in Wadbury Valley

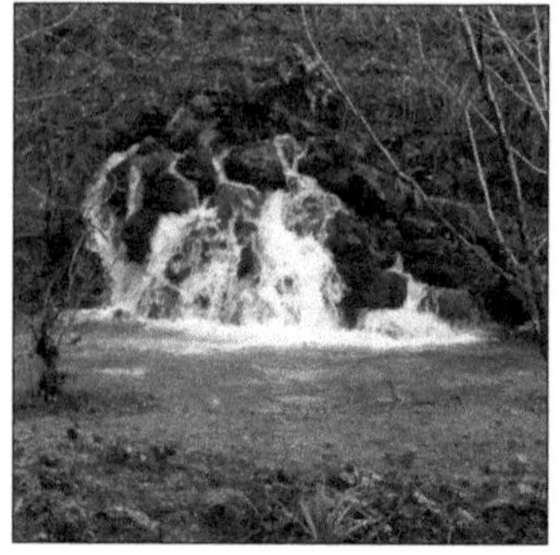

Outfall from Whatley quarry seen from the path beside Mells Stream

Now head diagonally to the R across a field to reach a gate to the L of a solitary oak tree in the hedgerow. Cross the track and enter the field opposite. Head up this tapering field until you reach a gated footbridge near the top L corner. Follow the hedgerow to your R. When to reach a double gate the right of way heads directly across the field towards the railway arch and a ST in the hedgerow opposite.

Now walk through the impressively built brick and stone railway arch – look out for the mysterious notice above.

You soon reach the village of Great Elm. Follow the lane as it joins a larger road at Old Chapel and continue past the former school to reach the Village Hall and Church of St Mary Magdalene on the R.

Carry on until you reach Manor Farm on your R and Elm Lodge on your L. Now head down the signposted bridleway to reach the path which follows the Mells Stream along the gorge-like Wadbury Valley, a damp habitat festooned with ferns, lichen and moss, and the very extensive ruins of Fussell's Edge Tool Works – all rather fascinating if slightly spooky. Another odd sight is the waterfall which apparently issues from the opposite bank. This is in fact water pumped from the base of a nearby stone quarry.

Wadbury Valley appears as a chasm in spectacular fashion beside an outcrop of Mountain Limestone as the path bears to the R to meet the road. Here turn L and head into Mells.

Note the roofed triangular construction at the road junction where a bench is provided which bears the inscription 'For the use of Mells village in memory of Mark Horner, 1908'. And on the opposite corner a splendid memorial to villagers who sacrificed their lives in two world wars. Mells is a village which possesses many features which make it especially memorable.

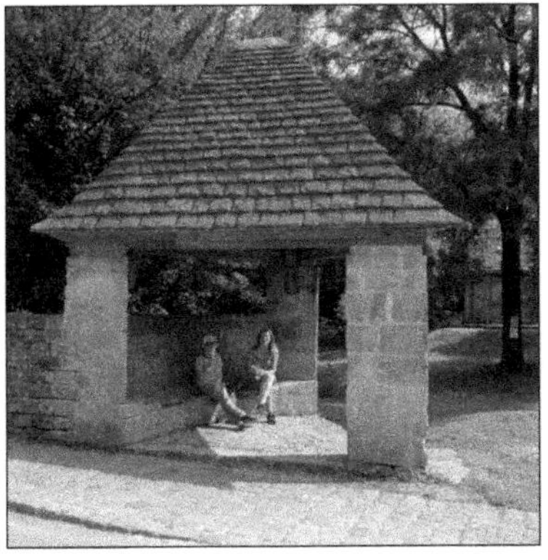

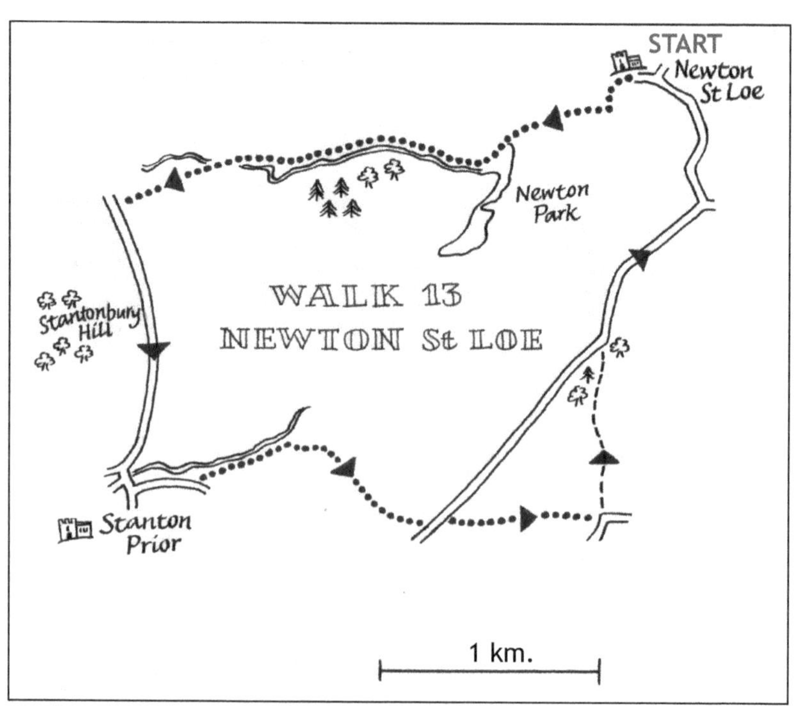

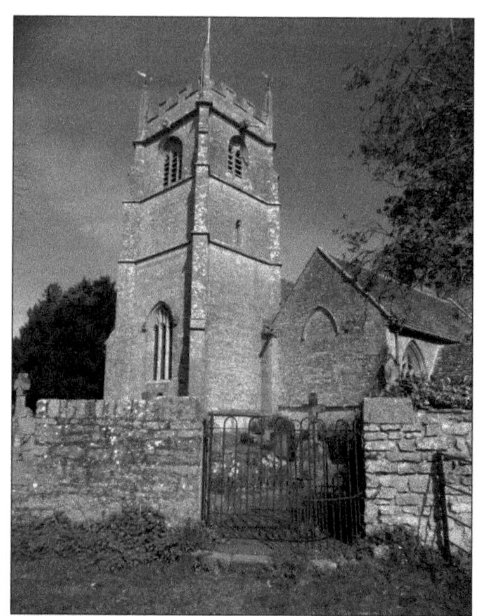

Holy Trinity church,
Newton St Loe

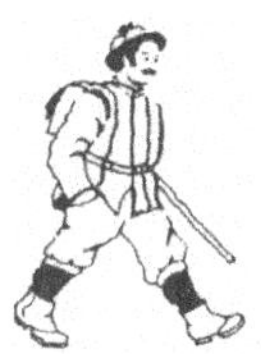

via Stantonbury Hill and Newton Park

Distance:	9¼ km. 5¾ miles
Map:	Explorer 155
Map reference:	649703
Refreshments en route:	Farm shop and café in Newton St Loe but nowhere en route. Stantonbury Hill might provide a good spot to picnic though this is a diversion from the route.

THE WALK is remarkably rural in character, given that it's so close to Bath. Newton St Loe is a village situated just south of the busy B-road which follows the southern edge of Bath via Odd Down and Combe Down and joins the A4 at the Corston roundabout west of the city. The village centre is marked by a small green triangle featuring a tree at its centre, surrounded by an uncomfortable-looking iron bench erected to commemorate the Queen's Silver Jubilee in 1977. The village Post Office is here also, together with a wall-mounted notice with information about the village.

DIRECTIONS

From the **green** at the centre of **Newton St Loe**, head along the lane, in a north-westerly direction, to the R of the house called **The Thatch**. Bear L at the junction of ways and head towards the church.

At the next minor junction, note the grand house on your L. This is the former Rectory which now serves as offices for the **Duchy of Cornwall** which is the landowner hereabouts - its arms are much in evidence on buildings in the course of this walk. Note also the former school, established in 1698 we are told, but not functioning as such since 1972.

Walk through the **churchyard** and leave it by a metal XG. Follow the fence down the slope, bear L and then R on reaching the lane. Carry on along the metalled path across a drive. From here, on looking R, you will spot the tower and tiny spire of **Corston church**, just half a mile from Newton St Loe's.

Continue in the same direction by following the path beside the pond, the fishing rights to which are robustly guarded by the Bathampton Angling Association. The buildings of Bath Spa University loom above.

Continue in the same direction by following the little stream up a delightful valley with sloping grassy flanks (featured across the title page of this book). You eventually forsake the stream to reach a XG in a top R-hand corner. Follow the hedge on your L to a second XG, passing an isolated old barn to your L.

Carry straight on - your view ahead is dominated by the wooded eminence of **Stantonbury Hill**. You swap a hedgerow to your L, via a plank bridge, to one to your R, by which you reach a lane. Here turn L.

> At a point where you are closest to the tree line on the eastern flank of the hill, where a line of trees descends to reach the lane, you are crossing the Wansdyke, though there is no visible evidence of this on the ground. There is, however, a gate on the R signposted as **Stantonbury Hill**, together with the Duchy logo (see opposite below).

Carry on along the lane, with the tower of Stanton Prior church in the distance, until you reach a minor junction.

> There is a PF sign indicating a beaten path which ascends the hill. The flattish open area atthe summit is peppered with pheasant feeders and hemmed in with trees so not much of interest. It may be worthwhile, however, to climb up as far as the tree line in order to take in the lovely view back across the valley in which lies the hamlet of Stanton Prior, complete with church.

From the junction carry on to the next turning on the L. The lane soon forks. You will see a PF sign showing a way between the forks and into the field ahead. Cross over and walk on by the beaten path on the L side of the field to reach a gate and footpath beside a stream.

Further along, at a XG, is a notice with a map showing permissive paths ahead, presumably by courtesy of the Duchy. Our course is now to

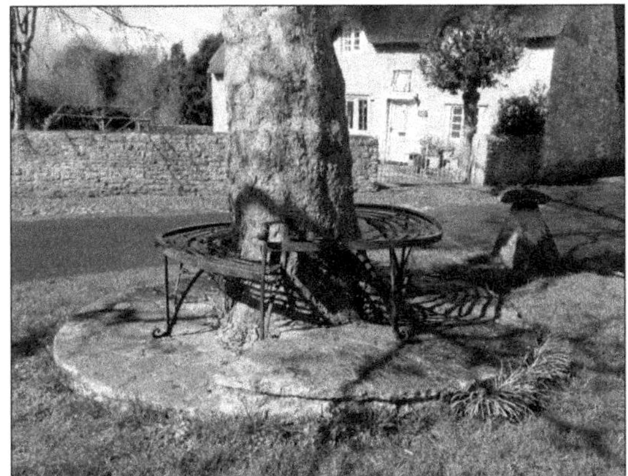

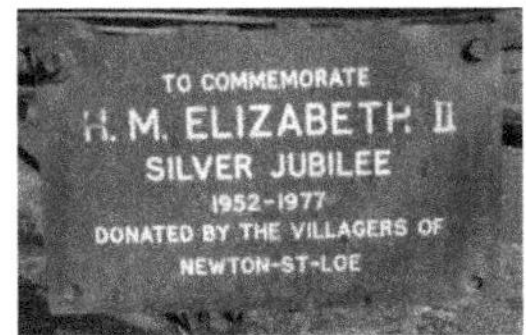

*Bench installed to com-
memorate the Silver Jubi-
lee in 1977 which encircles
a tree on the village green.*

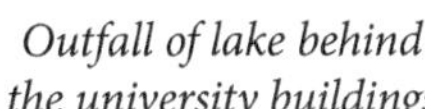

*Outfall of lake behind
the university buildings*

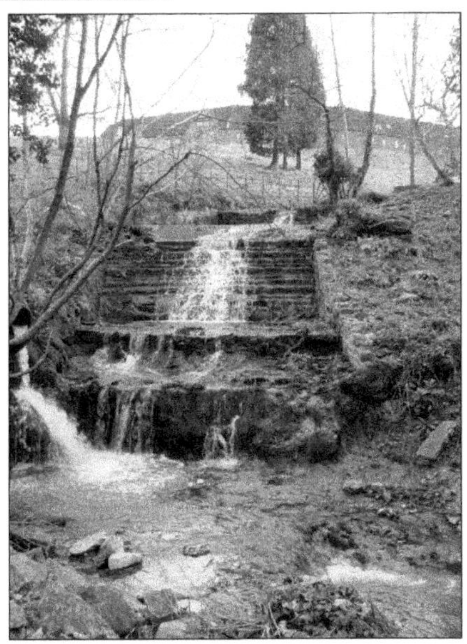

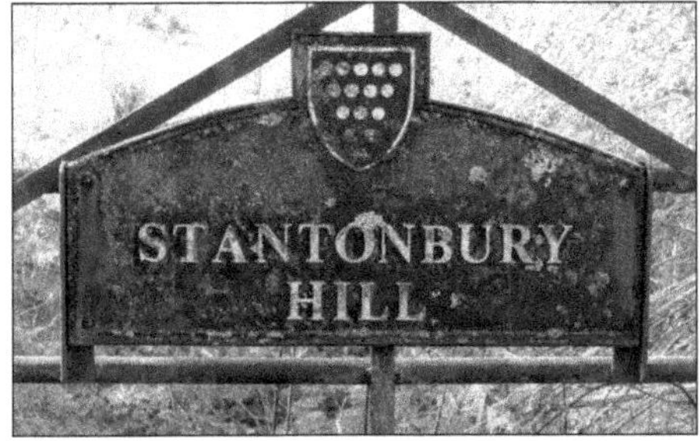

*Sign on gate indicating
Stantonbury Hill bearing the
arms of the Duchy of Cornwall*

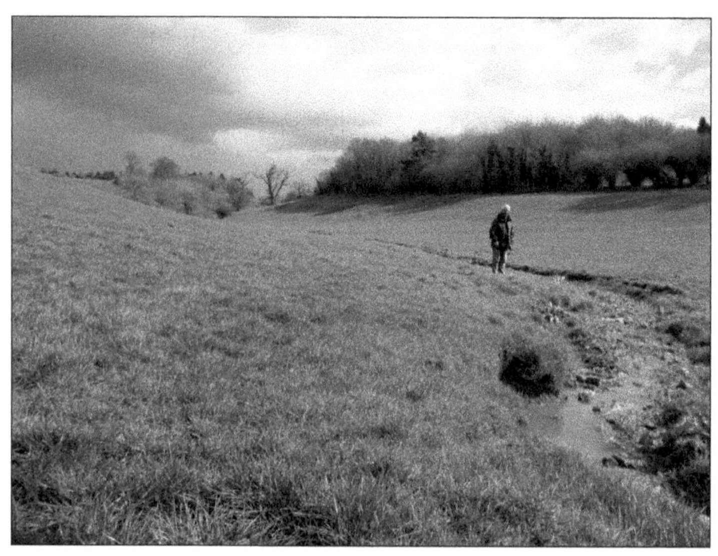

*The delightful shallow valley leading south-west from Newton St Loe;
see also the title page of this book*

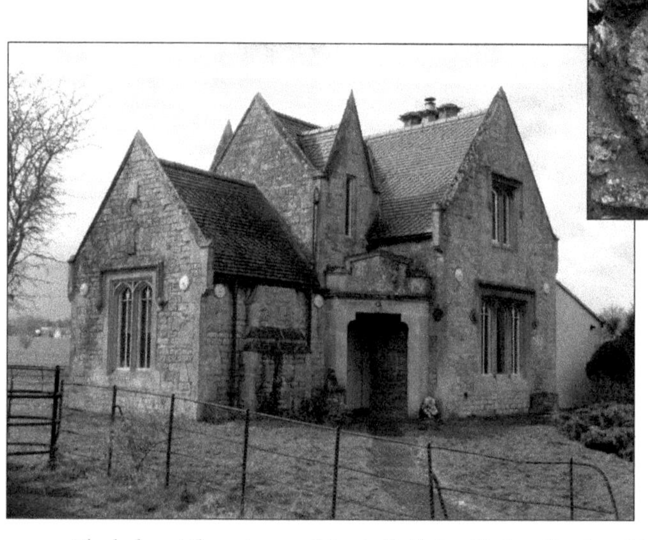

*The lodge at the entrance drive to Bath Spa University, closed to traffic,
and one of several fossil ammonites to be seen in the stone walls of
Newton St Loe; did you spot the one at the Lodge?*

follow the indicated way by ascending the slope with the field boundary to your R.

The ever expanding campus of Bath Spa University, distinguished at its centre by the imposing Georgian edifice of **Newton Park**, soon hoves into view. Pass through a XG.

The right of way cuts diagonally across this last field but, if there is a growing crop, it is perhaps advisable to follow the headland beside the hedge to your R. The boundary eventually curves to the L. When you reach a gate leading to Park Farm bear R towards a XG which drops you onto the lane.

At the road you can cut a corner to reach Newton St Loe by bearing L. However, to continue by the permissive access route, cross the lane directly to enter the field opposite. Follow the boundary to your L, then a second field until you reach a lane. Bear L here along an unmade track signposted as a Byway.

> Gaps in the hedge on your right will afford views towards the village of **Englishcombe** - so named because this was once an outpost of the English along the Wansdyke – surrounded by green fields. Further to the L and higher up you will see the massed ranks of houses at Twerton and Southdown.

On reaching the lane once more, bear R and carry on with views to your L towards the manor and church at Newton St Loe and further towards Kelston Park and Kelston Hill.

Take the first turning, downhill, on the L. This will lead you directly back to the village.

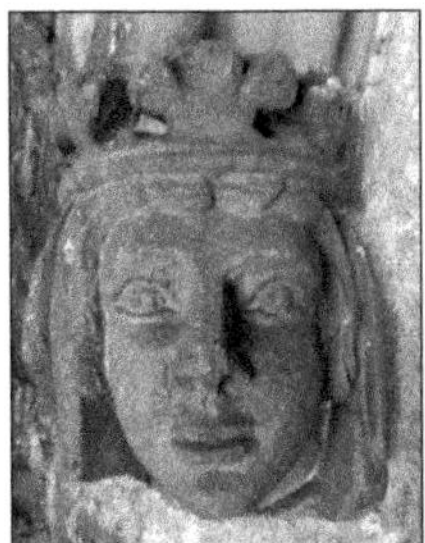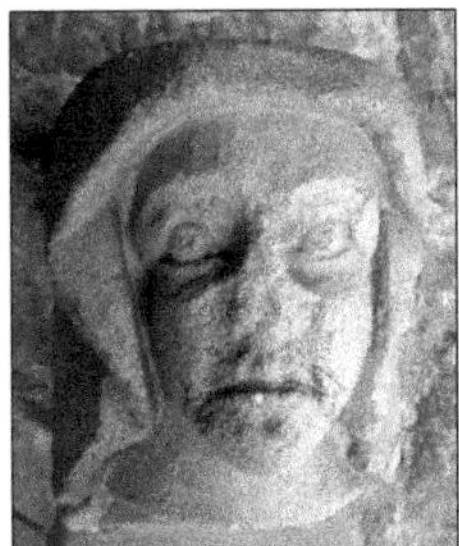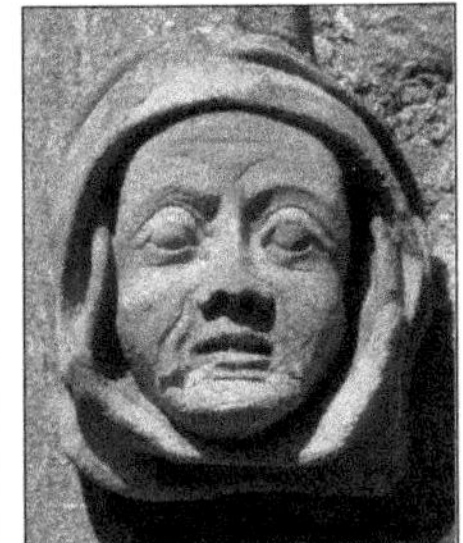

Three faces in stone from the church of St Peter and St Paul, Newton St Loe

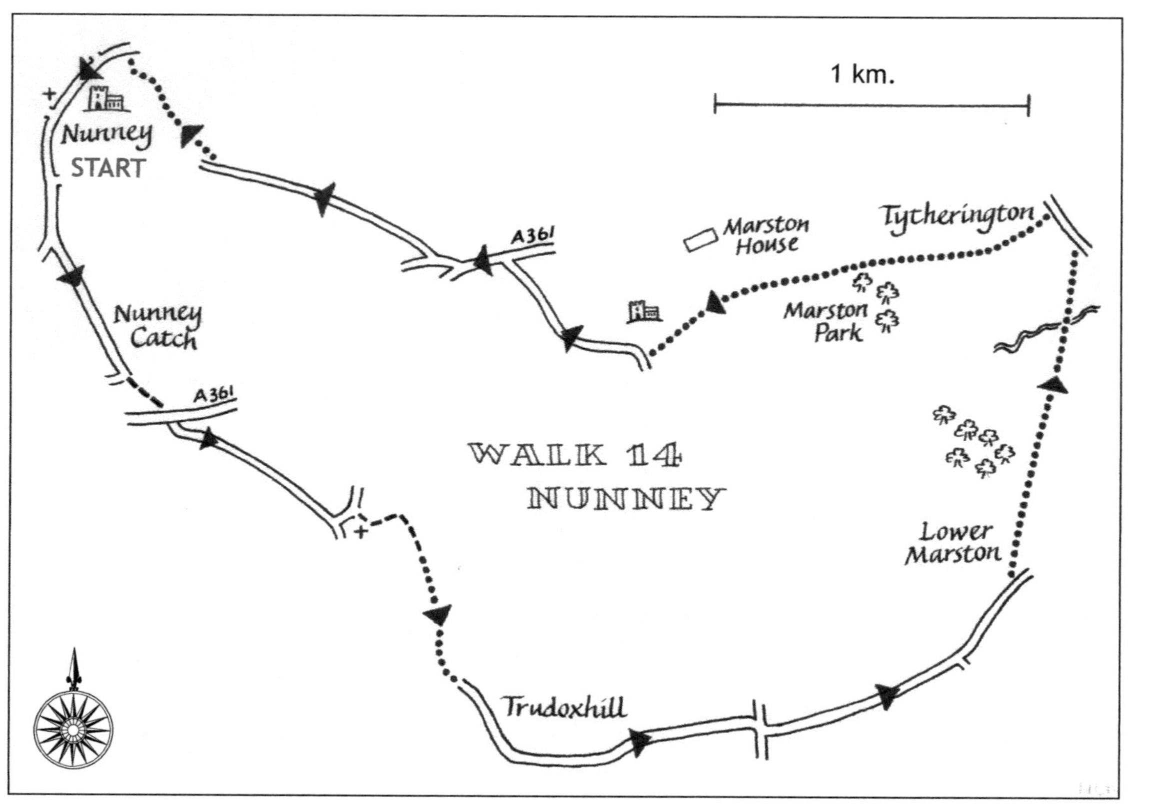

1 km.
Nunney START
Marston House
Tytherington
A361
Marston Park
Nunney Catch
A361
WALK 14 NUNNEY
Lower Marston
Trudoxhill

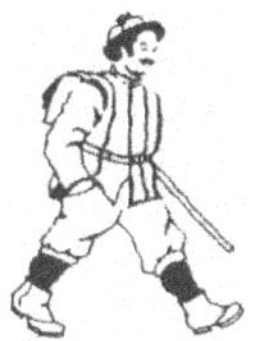

14 NUNNEY

via Trudoxhill, Tytherington, Marston House and Ridgeway

Distance:	10¾ km. 6¾ miles
Map:	Explorer 142
Map Reference:	456736
Refreshments en route:	The George pub, Moat and Turret café and shop in Nunney; The White Hart pub in Trudoxhill; Hen & Orchard in Tytherington

THE WALK is a varied one centred on the lovely village of Nunney which retains all the facilities once taken for granted in such communities: church, school, pub, shop and even a handy café. In addition the Nunney Brook enlivens the scene and feeds the moat which encloses the picturesque ruins of Nunney Castle. The ridge which separates Nunney to the north-west and Trudoxhill, Tytherington and Marston to the south-east and carries the busy A361 is negotiated by lane and footpath twice on this route but the ascents and descents are never harsh.

NOTE: The only possible inconvenience is crossing the A361 on the return leg to Nunney where due care is vital. Indeed, it may be advisable to tackle this route at the weekend when it is less frequented by heavy quarry traffic.

DIRECTIONS

From the centre of Nunney and with your back to the forecourt of the **SPAR shop**, bear R up the **High Street**. This becomes **Sunny Hill**. Take the L fork along **Catch Road** and continue past **Nunney First School**. At the

---

top of this road you will come to the former **Theobald Arms pub.**

Cross over and continue in the same direction by the track at the L side of the pub. As you approach the din of the busy A361, the track takes you beneath the road. Once you emerge on the far side bear L and begin a gentle descent. Turn L at the road.

At the junction below turn L into **Marl Pits Lane**. Very shortly turn R along the track. After bends L and R, look out for a PF sign indicating two rights of way. Go through the XG here and follow the hedge to your L. Then through a second XG and exit the next field by a XG in its far R corner by **Trudoxhill Village Hall.**

> You reach the road through the village opposite an old building with mullion windows - this is a chapel with small accompanying graveyard. You will find the **White Hart pub** a few yards to your R.

From the point where you join the street through the village turn L and soon leave the built-up area. On eventually reaching a minor crossroads continue by the lane signposted to Tytherington and Frome. Now the view opens up and you will soon spot the impressive façade of **Marston House** across fields to your L.

Once past **Burnt Cottage** and the junction of a lane which heads off to the R and indicated as No Through Road, look out for a PF sign beside a gate on your L. Go through here and bear R towards a 5-bar gate and footbridge across a stream. Next head for a ST at the corner of a wood. Cross a ditch by a pair of step stiles.

You must now strike a diagonal course across this field and in the same general direction of travel. When you reach a cross-track, the buildings of Tytherington hove into view though these are largely obscured when the trees are in leaf.

> Look around and notice that the surface of the field is marked by grooves and bumps - evidence that a former medieval village was situated here.

It is not easy to navigate the route from this point. Keep heading in the same general direction towards the tree line ahead. Don't head R, towards a gate, but to the L of a solitary tree at a point about thirty metres before the field boundary. If you head just to the L of this tree

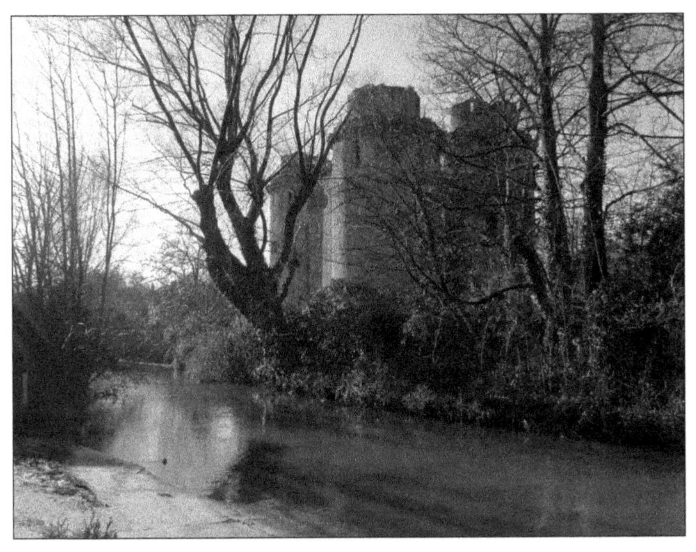

Nunney Castle viewed from Church Street

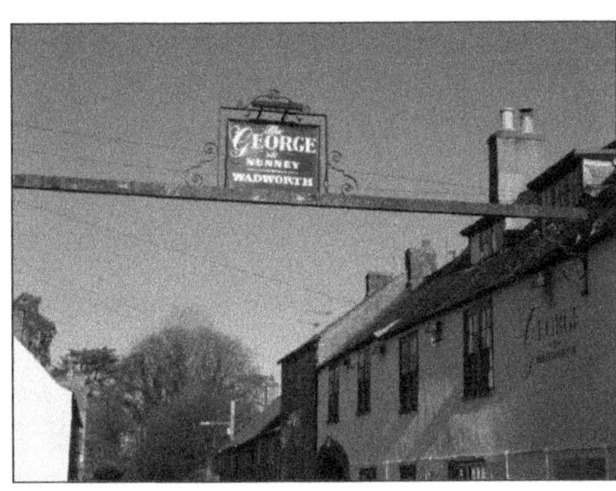

*The George pub sign
straddles the road*

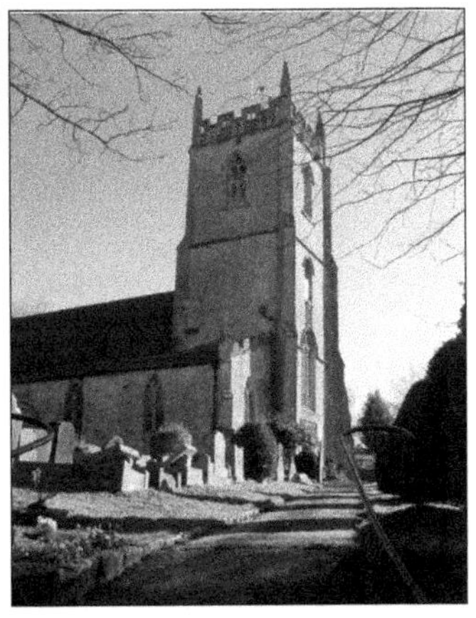

Approach to Nunney Church

you will locate a ST and footbridge. In the next field simply follow the beaten path to the R of a pond to reach a ST at the fence and then a stone ST onto the road at Tytherington where you will find the Hen & Orchard takeaway a short distance to the R.

To resume the walk: From the ST turn L, past the Lighthouse where you will spot a PF sign pointing L. Follow this way past the wood-clad buildings on your L and car park to reach a footbridge and gate.

Now follow the indicated permissive path beside the fence and towards the wood. Bear R until you reach a ST below the high brick wall. Cross over and follow a narrow fenced path to a further ST, then continue in the same direction.

You are following a course opposite and some distance from the boundary wall of **Marston House**. A number of direction posts indicate the way to join the lane somewhat to the L of **St Leonard's church** and its picturesque lych gate which you may wish to take a closer look at though it is generally kept locked.

Continue by ascending the lane to reach the A361 where you bear L by the pavement. After about a hundred metres you approach a turning on the opposite side. You must now cross the road - **<u>DO SO WITH GREAT CARE</u>**. Look both ways and when there is a suitable break in the flow of traffic make a dash for it.

Head down the turning opposite to the hamlet of **Ridgeway**. Bear R to descend **Ridgeway Lane** to the R of the postbox. Walk along this quiet way until you eventually reach the entrance gate to Byfield Cemetery on your L. Almost directly opposite is a signposted ST beside a gate. Cross here, then immediately cross another ST on your L which looks towards Nunney village, in particular the church tower and castle walls. Drop down to a ST near the opposite corner, then head to the R of a projecting hedgerow to reach a ST leading to a fenced path and on to Church Street. Turn L to reach The Market Square.

You will pass the market cross beside Nunney Brook, the entrance to the church, Nunney Castle and the SPAR shop.

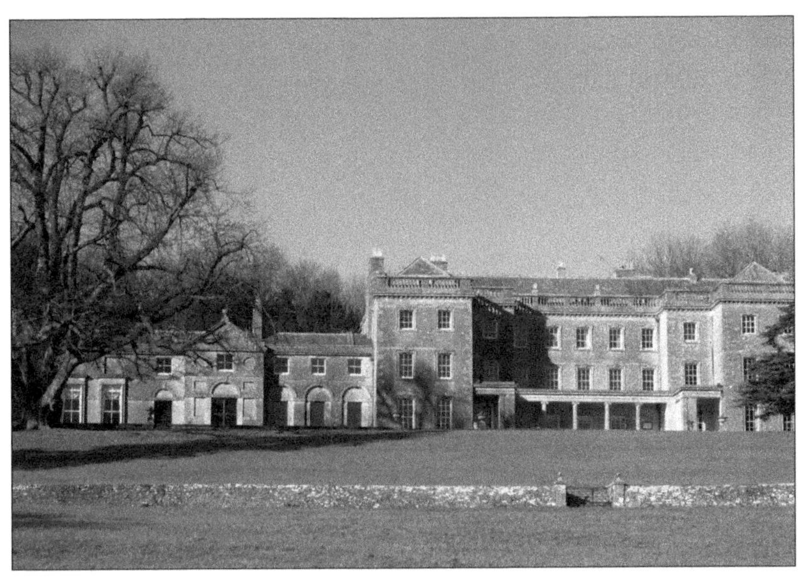

First recorded in the 17th Century, though much of its fabric is from the late 18th and early 19th centuries, Marston House has a chequered history. It was used by the US Army during World War 2 and was rescued from dereliction in 1984 when it became the company HQ of Foster Yeoman.

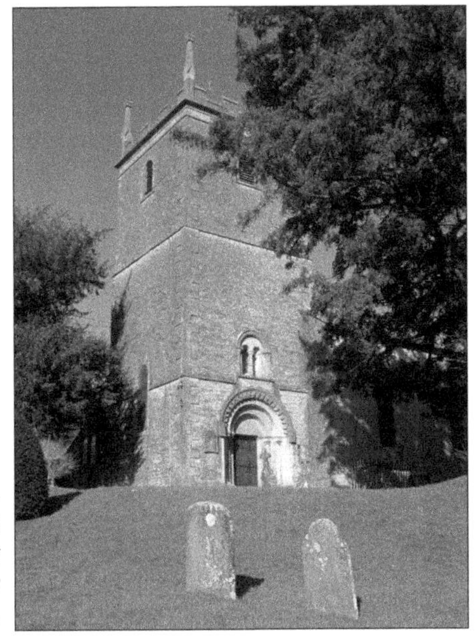

St Leonard's Church, Marston, dates from 1789 though it stands on the site of an earlier building and retains some 15th century stained glass.

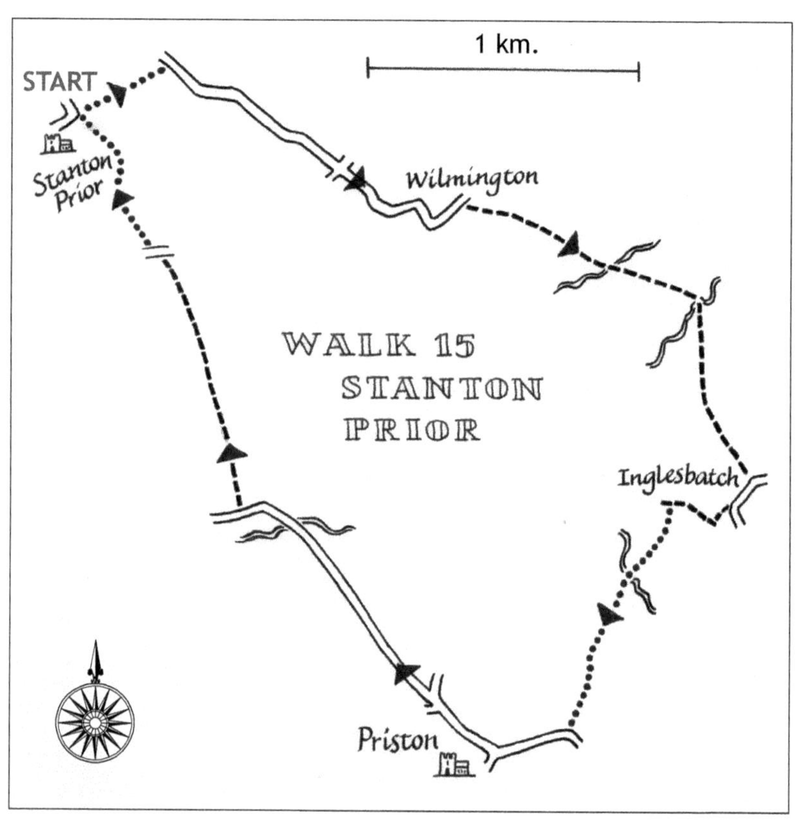

1 km.
START
Stanton Prior
Wilmington
WALK 15
STANTON
PRIOR
Inglesbatch
Priston

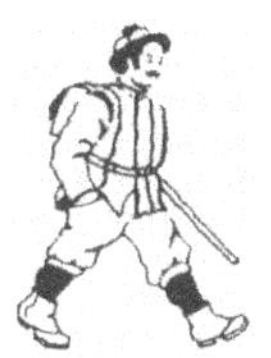

15 STANTON PRIOR

via Wilmington, Inglesbatch and Priston

Distance:	8 km. 5 miles
Map:	Explorer 155
Map reference:	694605
Refreshments en route:	The Ring o' Bells pub in Priston

THE WALK is an invigorating one across hills and valleys which offers wide views across the uncrowded rural hinterland. As expected, hills and valleys mean ups and downs: there is a steady ascent by lane to Wilmington crossroads, then a long descent to cross Newton Brook, then up again to Inglesbatch. Priston is a little more than half way and makes a good spot to take a break before another steady ascent and final descent to return to the starting point. This route traverses land belonging to the Duchy of Cornwall whose arms you will spot many times en route.

DIRECTIONS

To begin the walk: With your back to little **St Lawrence church** in Stanton Prior bear R to a minor junction (where there is usually space to park a car). Look for the PF signs opposite and follow the direction of the rightward pointing sign via the beaten path across the field towards a ST in the hedgerow opposite. Now carry on across a second field to reach the lane where you turn R.

Walk along this quiet way and begin to climb until you reach a ridge-top crossroads with a sign indicating **Wilmington** ¼ straight across. As you pass **Wilmington Farm** the view opens out until you reach the few dwellings which comprise the hamlet. You pass a PF sign on your right which provides a direct way to Priston. Our route, however, is reached a few yards further, immediately past the postbox, where you bear R by way of a hedged track which provides a steady descent across a couple of streams, then a climb to emerge at the hamlet of **Inglesbatch.**

On reaching the lane turn R and pass a former chapel, 'The Chantry', where you bear R and R again at **Home Farm/The Spud Shop.** Now begin to descend by a track which serves a number of dwellings. Just past a pig unit, where the metalled track runs out, keep your eyes peeled for a little wooden gate beside a farmgate.

Go through here and, after a few yards, pass through a XG to enter a field and enjoy a wide view with the tower of Priston Church directly ahead. Follow the fenced path and head downhill. Reach a further XG, then head straight on towards a gate which leads you via a footbridge across a stream.

Now follow the field edge on your L but keep alert for a XG which leads through a patch a woodland above the stream via a second XG, then beside **Priston Sewage Treatment Works** to reach the lane where you bear R – you will once again spot the tower of St Luke's church – to reach the centre of **Priston.**

Keep bearing R until you reach the green triangle outside the **Ring O' Bells pub** and **Village Hall.** From here you can reach the church by bearing L, then L at the fork and finally R.

To continue the walk: With your back to the pub, walk up the lane opposite, then take the R fork which is signposted to **Priston Mill ½.** Just a few metres further along, take the L fork and walk on until you cross Conygre Brook – a tributary of Newton Brook which we crossed before the climb up to Inglesbatch.

On the far side, the lane begins to climb. The lane levels out as it bears L. You reach a cluster of buildings on your R. Here you turn sharp R to follow the bridleway as it ascends the slope between fields. Simply carry on until you finally crest the ridge and reach a lane.

Cross over the slightly staggered crosstrack to reach the final stage of the walk by an enclosed byway which leads you down to **Stanton Prior.** At a gap in the hedge on the R you will be able to look towards Newton St Loe, distinguished by the tower of Holy Trinity church.

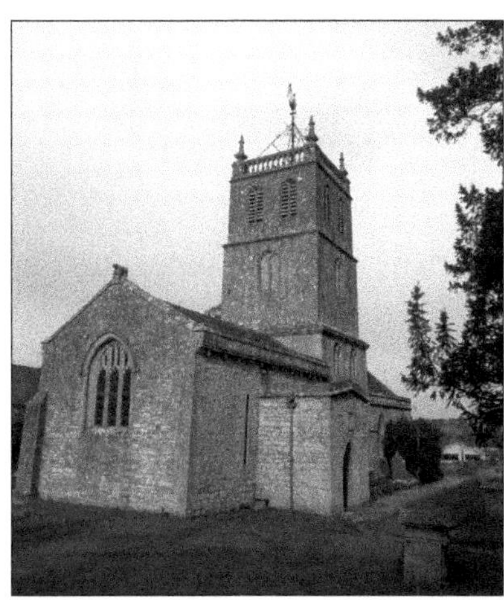

St Lawrence church in Stanton Prior: a simple nave, chancel, tower and porch

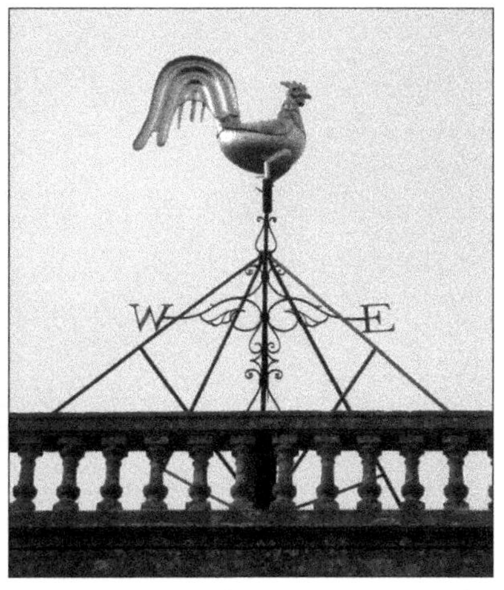

The cockerel weathervane, 200 years old, perched atop the tower of St Luke's church in Priston

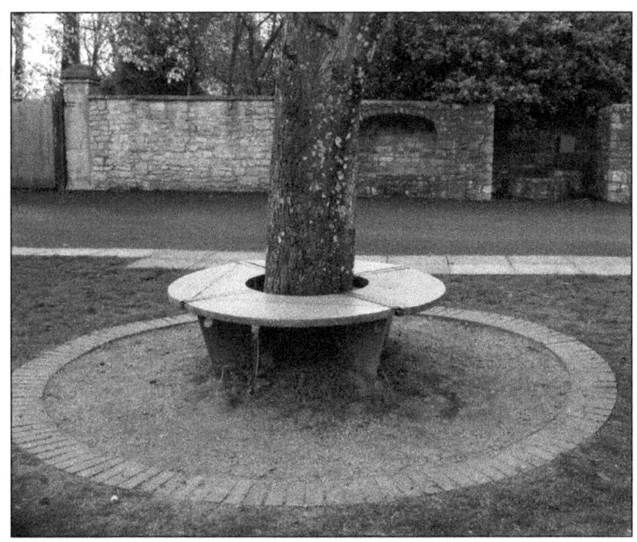

Bench on the small green outside the Ring o' Bells in Priston – be sure to read the inscriptions here

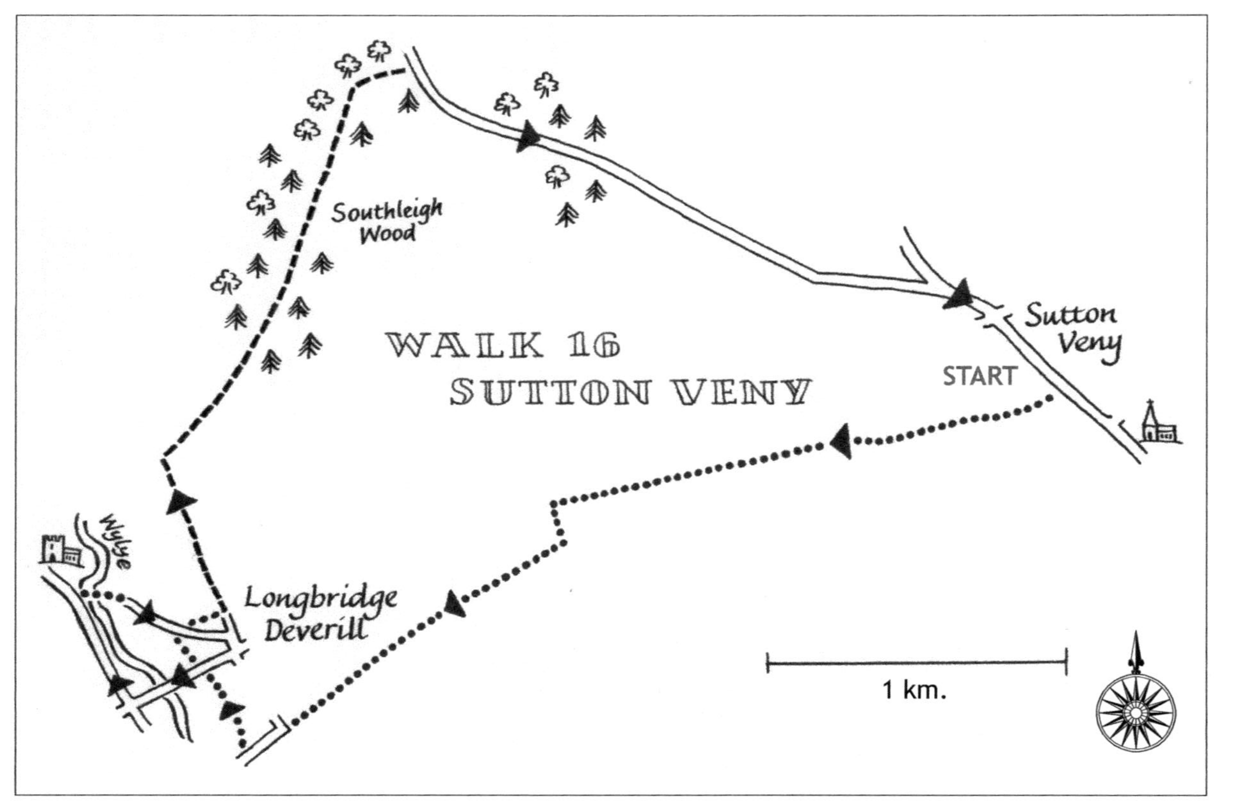

Southleigh Wood
WALK 16
SUTTON VENY
START
Sutton Veny
Wylye
Longbridge Deverill
1 km.

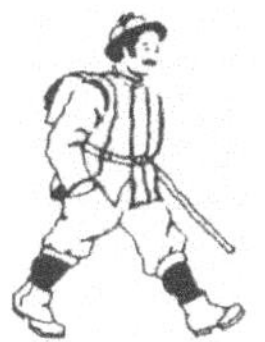

16 SUTTON VENY

via Longbridge Deverill

Distance:	10¼ km. 6¾ miles
Map:	Explorer 143
Map reference:	422898
Refreshments en route:	The Woolpack pub in Sutton Veny; The George in Longbridge Deverill

THE WALK is fairly level throughout, so no hill climbs. Like many of the walks described in this book, it links a couple of villages, and the routes to and from Sutton Veny and Longbridge Deverill follow a pleasant mix of quiet lanes, woodland tracks and field paths. As ever, there are points of interest in the villages visited. In Longbridge Deverill, for example, you could opt for a slightly longer route which takes in the George pub, the village church and almshouses and River Wylye. This short detour is shown as a boxed section in the route description overleaf.

DIRECTIONS

At the central crossroads in Sutton Veny you will find the Woolpack Inn. Begin the walk by facing the **Woolpack** pub and turn left along the main Street through the village. The imposing spire of the church will soon come into view. Look out for the entrance to **Dymocks Lane** on your R. Just past here is a series of **concrete bollards** at an unsigned opening, also on your R.

Turn in here and follow a straight course for around a mile first by a fenced path and then via a series of field crossings and to the rear of the Deverill Road Industrial Estate, consisting of single-storey former army huts. The fine view and shapely outline to your left follows the slope of Longbridge Hill rising to Cow Down.

You eventually reach the range of buildings at **Long Ivor Farm**. Turn L immediately past here beside cattle sheds, stables and riding school. Pass through a gate and then another on your R to regain the same south-westerly direction first beside a hedge to your L, then to your R, to reach **Longbridge Deverill**. Join the road and head on between houses.

Look out for **Number 38** on your L, almost opposite which there is the entrance by a gate to a narrow field between dwellings (if you reach a watercourse you will have passed it). Follow the field boundary on your R to reach a XG, then a further XG to exit between houses onto the main street through the village.

ALTERNATIVE DETOURS to church and/or pub - an extra half mile

If you wish only to visit the church - and avoid walking beside the busy A350 - head across the road through the village to the L of Owl Cottage. Look for the enclosed footpath just to the L of the drive. Head along here until you reach a lane where you bear L and gradually descend to a field and footbridge across the clear and fast-flowing River Wylye.

You will spot the church tower on your R. Head towards it by bearing R beside the Almshouses and past the Parish Hall.

If you wish to visit the **George pub** and then perhaps head on to the village church, turn left, walk to the main road and cross over - with care.

Having visited or bypassed the pub and you wish to continue to the church, cross back over the main road - the busy A350 - where, thankfully, you will find a pavement which will take you to the **church of St Peter and St Paul** with its various monuments to the Thynne family of Longleat. Note also the plough to the right of the porch, a plough made by Reeves of Bratton (see Walk 4). In April/May there is a stunning blossom on the Judas tree to the L of the porch and, in February, a carpet of snowdrops. Just before the church you will pass the attractive almshouses known as **Sir James Thynne House.**

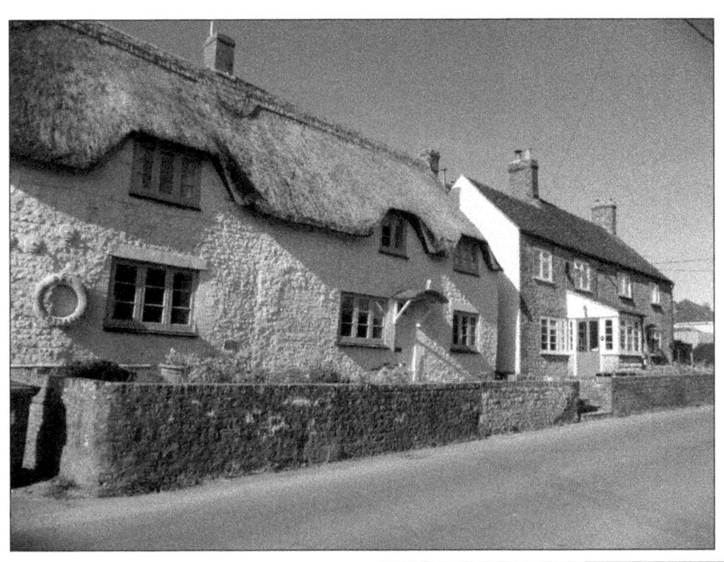

Cottages in Longbridge Deverill

*St Peter and St Paul Church,
Longbridge Deverill*

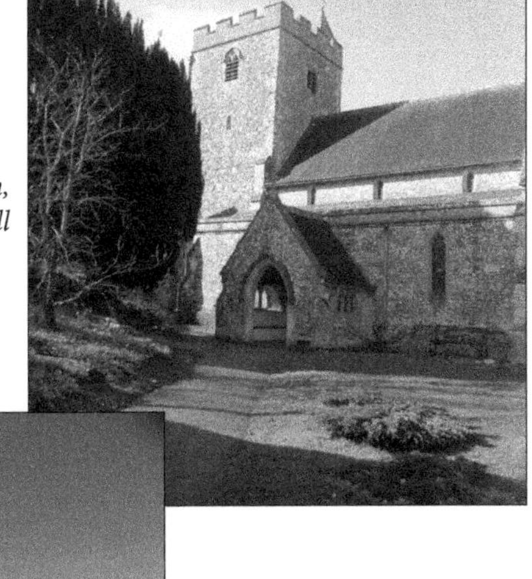

*Almshouses in Longbridge
Deverill, founded in 1655
and known as Sir James
Thynne House. It provides
accommodation for six
elderly folk but its prominent
clock is not entirely reliable*

If you don't wish to visit the pub and/or church, cross the village street and take the footpath beside **Owl Cottage**. Carry on until you reach a lane where you turn R and, after a few yards, reach a field opening and ST.

Cross here and bear R to cross a second ST. Now turn L on reaching the track, signposted as a bridleway. You reach a gate to enter a field. Bear half-R beside the raised Sandhill Reservoir to reach a gate which leads into **Southleigh Wood**. This is a contrasting but enjoyable section of the walk.

The trees are mixed deciduous and coniferous, including some magnificently tall larches, which grow haphazardly and not planted in regimented rows. There is plenty of light penetrating the branches and especially along the track you are following.

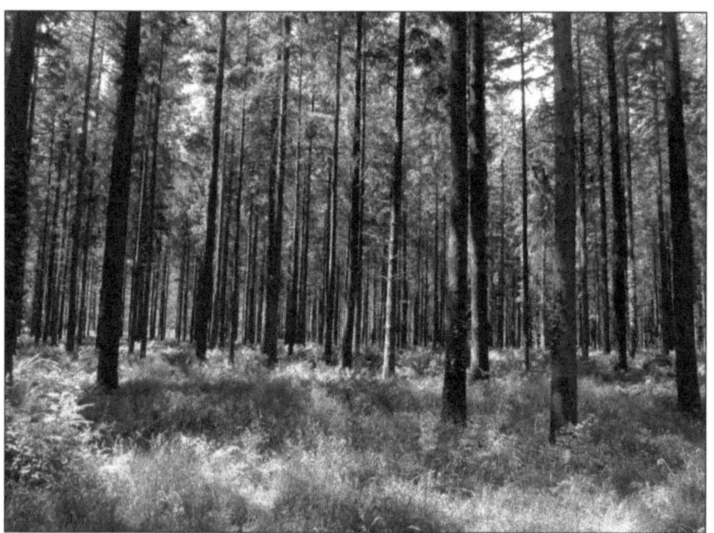

Sky-scraping conifers in Southleigh Wood

You eventually reach **Five Ash Lane** where you turn R to follow it all the way back to the junction in **Sutton Veny** where you began. This is a metalled lane openly accessible but is little frequented by vehicular traffic. At the village crossroads bear R to reach the **Woolpack Inn.**

If you wish to explore further, and if you have time it is recommended to do so, carry on as far as the church and the war graves. Further on again is a lane on the left signposted to the abandoned St Leonard's church.

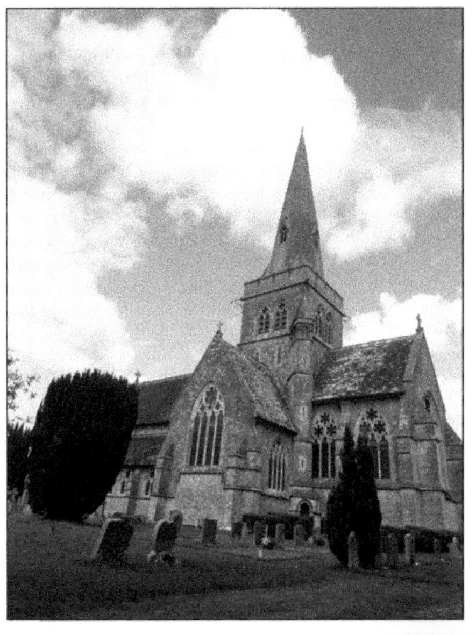

St John Evangelist Church Sutton Veny founded in 1866 and built in the Early English style

Commonwealth war graves in the churchyard

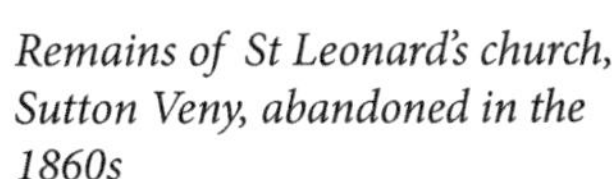

Remains of St Leonard's church, Sutton Veny, abandoned in the 1860s

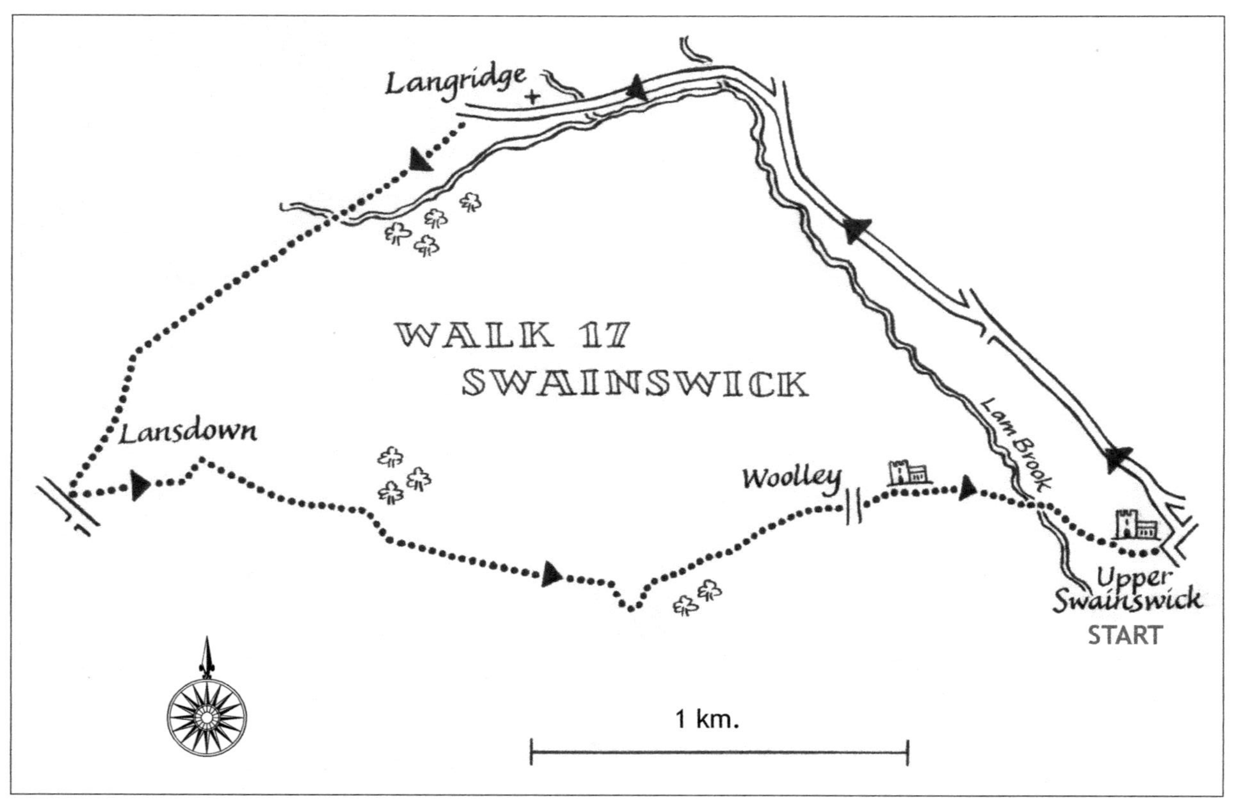
Langridge
Lansdown
WALK 17
SWAINSWICK
Woolley
Lam Brook
Upper
Swainswick
START
1 km.

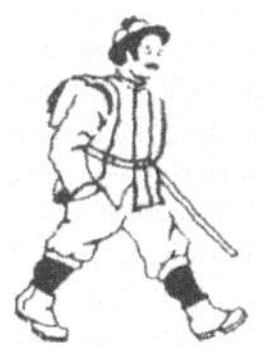

17 SWAINSWICK

via Langridge, Lansdown and Woolley

Distance:	8 km. 5 miles
Map:	Explorer 155
Map reference:	684757
Refreshments en route:	The Blathwayt Arms, Lansdown

THE WALK, though not many miles, is demanding of effort. There is a steep climb through around 500 feet to the summit of Lansdown, then a sharp descent to Woolley and the valley bottom. It is possible to complete the route in a couple of hours with the occasional break to catch your breath. On the other hand, you may decide to stop at the natural half-way point on Lansdown to enjoy refreshment at the Blathwayt Arms.

DIRECTIONS

From **Swainswick** take the lane just above the church signposted to Tadwick. Walk along here away from the village and enjoy the wide views across the valley to the slope opposite and the village of Woolley distinguished by its Georgian church with prominent belfry - the walk returns this way – though in summer it is obscured by trees in leaf.

Ignore the lane signposted to **Woolley** on the L but continue until the lane forks - take the L fork beside **Ashcombe Farm** signposted to **Langridge**. You follow Lam Brook for a short distance but continue beside a tributary stream which flows down the steep valley to your L.

The way ascends steadily. Langridge – the long ridge – is aptly named. You will soon find the **little church of St Mary Magdalene**, an ancient edifice set in a neatly-walled churchyard. It consists of nave, chancel and saddle-back tower with an interesting interior.

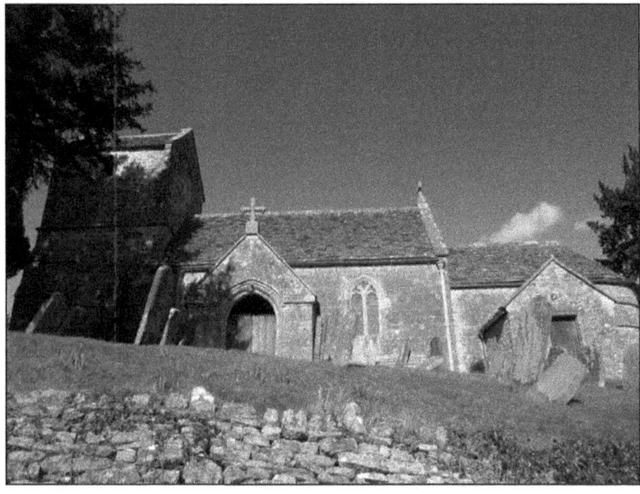

Looking up from the lane to the little church of St Mary Magdalene, Langridge, which dates from the 12th century and was restored by the Victorians. Look out for a rare figure of the Virgin and Child set above the chancel arch.

Continue climbing until, just past **Court Farm**, look out for a PF on your L. Head through the XG and follow the fence on your R to a second XG. Cross the field and descend to the bottom L corner to a signposted PF leading to a stream. Cross here and bear R to tackle the stiff climb beside the field boundary to your R to reach a XG.

Head straight on, still ascending, with a view across the valley on your R towards the buildings of Langridge. You can also look back in an easterly direction towards the skyline and the constant flow of traffic on the A46 Gloucester Road.

The exit from this field is not the wide farm gate which you will see ahead, but a slab ST set in the stone wall some 100 metres to its L. Cross here and, as you approach the driveway a short distance ahead you will find a signpost indicating the PF to Langridge Church back the way you have come.

To continue the walk, omitting the Blathwayt Arms at the main road across Lansdown: head directly across the field to reach a stone slab stile and accompanying PF sign.

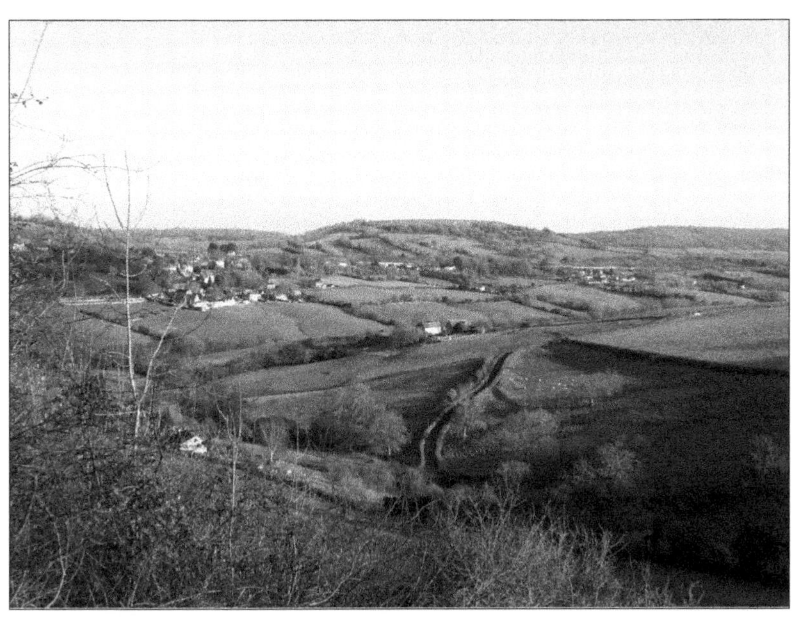

Panoramic view across St Catherine's Valley towards Charmy Down

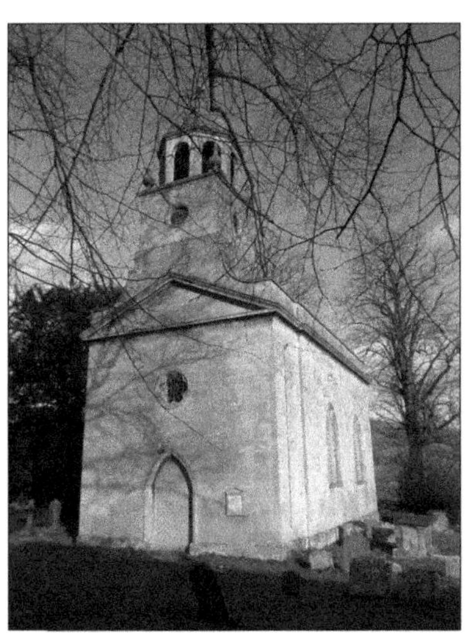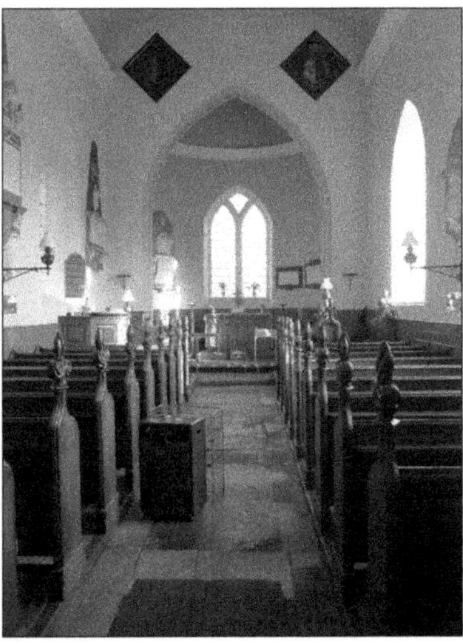

Exterior and interior of the Georgian church of All Saints at Woolley

If you wish to visit the Blathwayt Arms then head on along the drive until you reach the road. The **racecourse** is evident on the far side – and the **Blathwayt Arms** a little way along to your R.

To continue the walk: From the main road and the driveway to Upper Langridge Farm: cross the cattle grid and head off across the field in a half-R direction, between the first and second posts, towards a stone slab ST and accompanying PF sign in the field boundary.

Cross here and bear L, then R, across a stone ST and finally a wooden XG at a scrapyard. Bear R here, then L to cross the drive and continue by path. Enter a field and follow the beaten path a little to the L. Note the singular **Beckford Tower** away to your R, all 146 feet of it. Cross a couple more stone STs, then begin gradually to descend.

Make for the far boundary to reach a Bristol gate. The way now is signed at the Circuit of Bath. Once through the gate you begin the steep descent made clear by a series of steps and indicator posts.

You reach a rudimentary wooden bench beside the path which is an ideal spot to savour the wide and distant view across the Lambrook valley. The path eventually opens out and grows a little less steep as you descend towards Woolley.

Simply carry on, still descending. You will spot the bell tower of the church though it is likely to be obscured by trees in the summer. Exit the field to reach a drive. Bear R, then L and R again along Church Street. As you approach the church gate note the stone ST leading to a footpath just to the R.

All Saints church is not your typical ancient village church, so do venture in. It was rebuilt in 1761 to a design by John Wood the Younger.

To continue, head down the path beside the boundary wall of the churchyard, then enter a field. Carry on descending to reach the bottom-most corner where you cross a bridge over Lam Brook. This point marks the end of the long descent from Lansdown - somewhere in excess of 500 feet.

Bear R towards a XG, then traverse the hillside below the buildings of Swainswick to reach steps leading to a gate with a notice warning that you are about to take a right of way through a private garden. Make haste to reach the lane beside the village church of **St Mary's**, nestling peacefully in its walled churchyard.

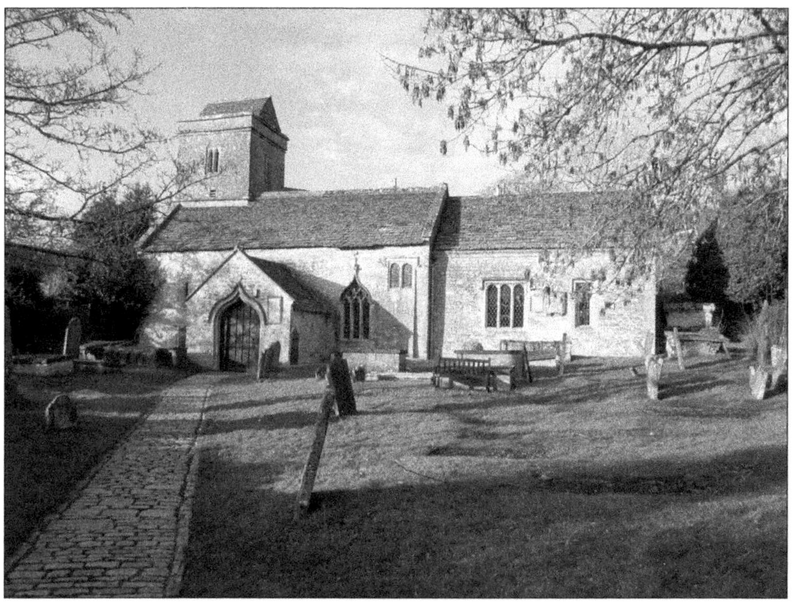

Church of St Mary in Swainswick

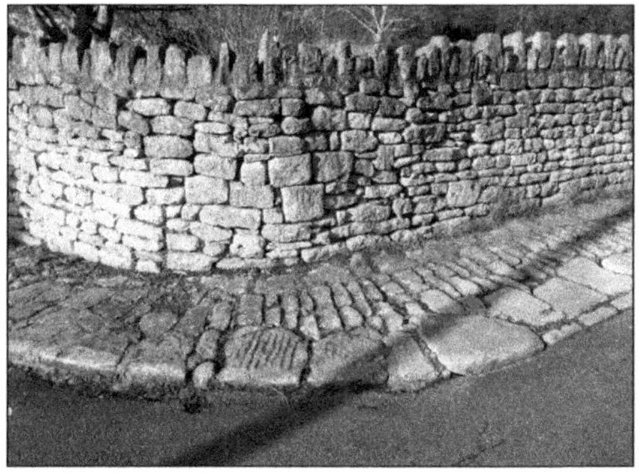

Stone wall and stone sett pavement wrapped around the churchyard at Swainswick

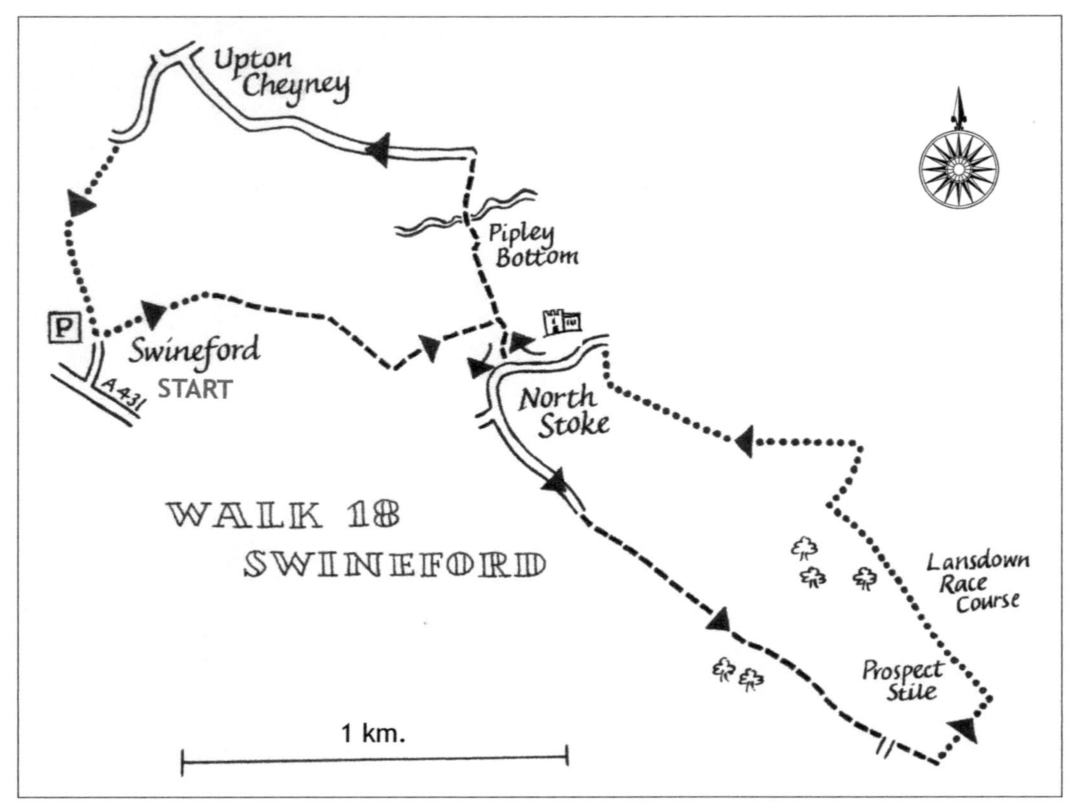

Upton
Cheyney
Pipley
Bottom
P
Swineford
START
A431
North
Stoke
WALK 18
SWINEFORD
Lansdown
Race
Course
Prospect
Stile
1 km.

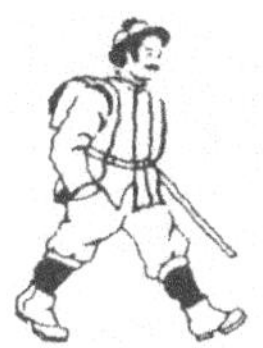

18 SWINEFORD

via North Stoke, Prospect Stile, Lansdown and Upton Cheyney

Distance:	8 km. 5 miles
Map:	Explorer 155
Map reference:	691691
Refreshments en route:	Pubs - The Swan at Swineford; Upton Inn in Upton Cheyney

THE WALK is a challenging one, though not over-long. There is a steady rise across fields and along a bridleway between Swineford and North Stoke and later a sharp ascent to reach the 230 metre high point at Prospect Stile – that's a rise of around 220 metres (720 feet) from start. Soon after there is a downhill section with glorious and far-reaching views to return to North Stoke. On leaving that village there is a steep and rocky descent to Pipley Bottom followed by a gentler climb up on the far side. This walk definitely calls for walking boots!

Both North Stoke and Upton Cheyney are just across the Somerset border and lie in South Gloucestershire, though both close to Bath.

DIRECTIONS

Swineford lies on the main A431 road which connects Bath and Bristol at a point where it touches the River Avon. There is a pub, The Swan, facing the road and a brown sign indicating SWINEFORD Picnic Area and Parking. This is the starting and finishing point of the walk.

At the entrance to the car park you will see a signpost indicating public footpaths in three directions. Take the one pointing to an open field beyond.

Head across to meet a XG signposted to North Stoke. Continue in the same direction towards a high point where you will find another XG. This leads to a hedged path – actually a bridleway – by which you continue to gain height. Continue on the main track, passing a footpath to your R. Eventually you reach a signposted meeting of ways. Bear R here, up the stony track - on your R is the **Coach House** with stables and a four-step **mounting block** - towards the buildings of **North Stoke.**

At the T-junction turn R. The lane soon bears to the L and then heads off downhill to the R. At this point carry on in the same direction, gaining height once more.

The track levels out and gives wide views to the south and west across the River Avon, Bitton, Keynsham and Dundry Hill to the south of Bristol. The tree-clad summit of Kelston Hill is ahead of you, a little to the right.

The way grows more enclosed and begins to rise once again. You reach a XG, then a cross- track and, a little further on, a high wooden XG on your left bearing a sign indicating the route of the **Cotswold Way.** Bear L here, through the gate and climb uphill.

At the top of the climb you reach **Prospect Stile** (which is, in fact, a XG).

From Prospect Stile there is, not surprisingly, a great prospect. There is also a toposcope which will assist you, on a clear day, to identify various landmarks. The most distant is Alfred's Tower at 33km. To the west is the Severn Estuary and to the east Westbury White Horse.

From Prospect Stile the route takes you back in a westerly direction. So, with your back to the toposcope, bear L to follow the hedge on your L.

As you do so, you will see that you are following the edge of the Lansdown plateau and that the land to your L drops away steeply. On your R is **Lansdown Race Course**.

Go through a XG to reach a boundary where you are directed R and then L into a wide field with a distinct path through it and a huge view ahead.

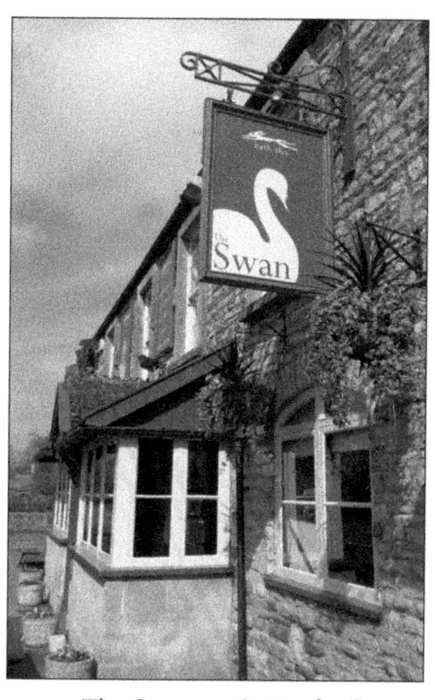

The Swan at Swineford

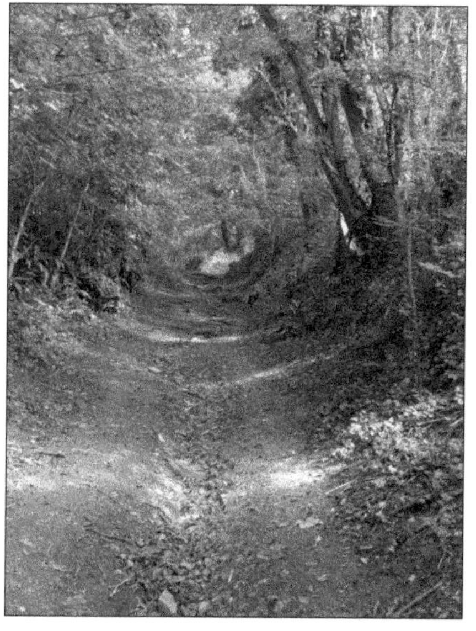

*Bridleway, sun-dappled here,
en route to North Stoke*

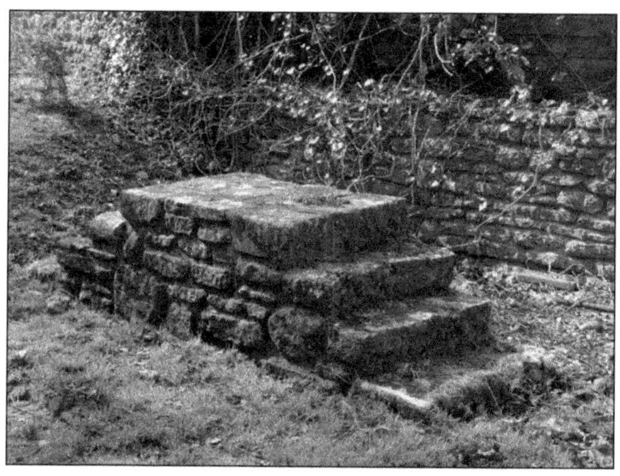

Fine mounting block on approach to North Stoke

The distinctive red brick edifice of the former Fry's Chocolate factory, now redeveloped as 'The Chocolate Quarter' on the northern edge of Keynsham is prominent in the half distance.

You will spot the pinnacles surmounting the tower of **North Stoke Church** below and to the R. Descend the slope by the beaten path in more or less the same direction and descend towards a cluster of farm buildings. Look out for a direction post which points you to the R, towards a ST and gate in the far L corner. Cross the ST and bear L through the churchyard.

You will pass the elegant North Stoke Millennium Bench (see opposite) which invites you to sit and take in the expansive view which, on a clear day, will include the Welsh mountains.

Head down the **church steps** with care to reach the lane through the village. This can be a watery spot but there is a raised pavement on the far side.

Turn R at **Chestnut Barn** - you will recognise this as the route you took on reaching North Stoke from Upton Cheyney earlier. At the now familiar junction of ways further along, take the R-hand course **along the Bridleway, not the indicated PF**. This offers a steep, rocky and often watery descent to reach a concrete slab bridge across a stream, a spot indicated on the Explorer map as **Pipley Bottom**.

The path on the far side climbs, less steeply, to meet an open track. Turn L here and follow the undulating way to return to **Upton Cheyney**. There is a short cut by an indicated PF back to Swineford but, for the sake of visiting another village, continue along the lane to reach a junction.

Turn L downhill, past the minor junction and the impressive bench seat, built as a First World War memorial. **Upton Inn** is on your R.

Carry on downhill via a R-hand bend. Look out for the **second** opening on the L. There is a PF sign here, attached to a post, though it is not easy to spot. It indicates the path downhill towards **Swineford**. Now simply follow the beaten path via a XG, hedgerows and final wide views - the tower of Bitton church visible in the foreground - to reach your starting point at **Swineford**.

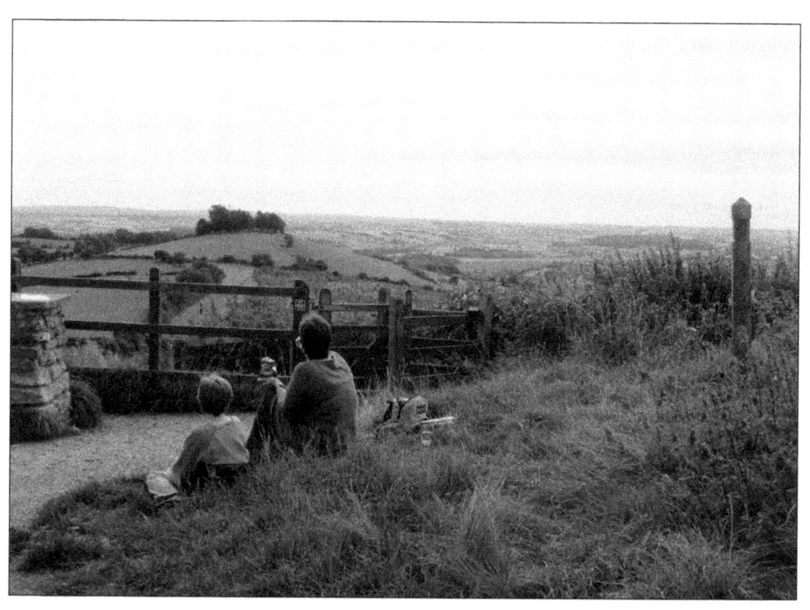

At Prospect Stile and looking towards Kelston Hill

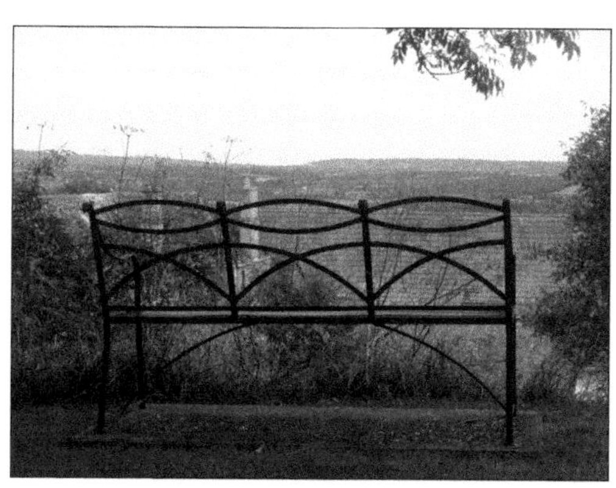

*Millennium bench in churchyard at
North Stoke facing west*

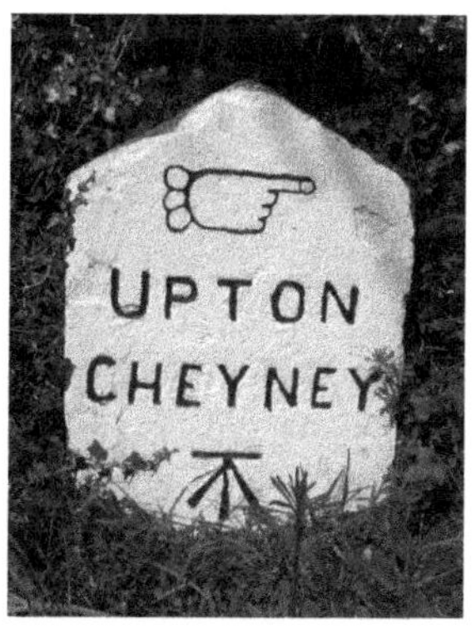

*Attractive direction
marker, with manicule,
on the A431
Bath-Bristol road*

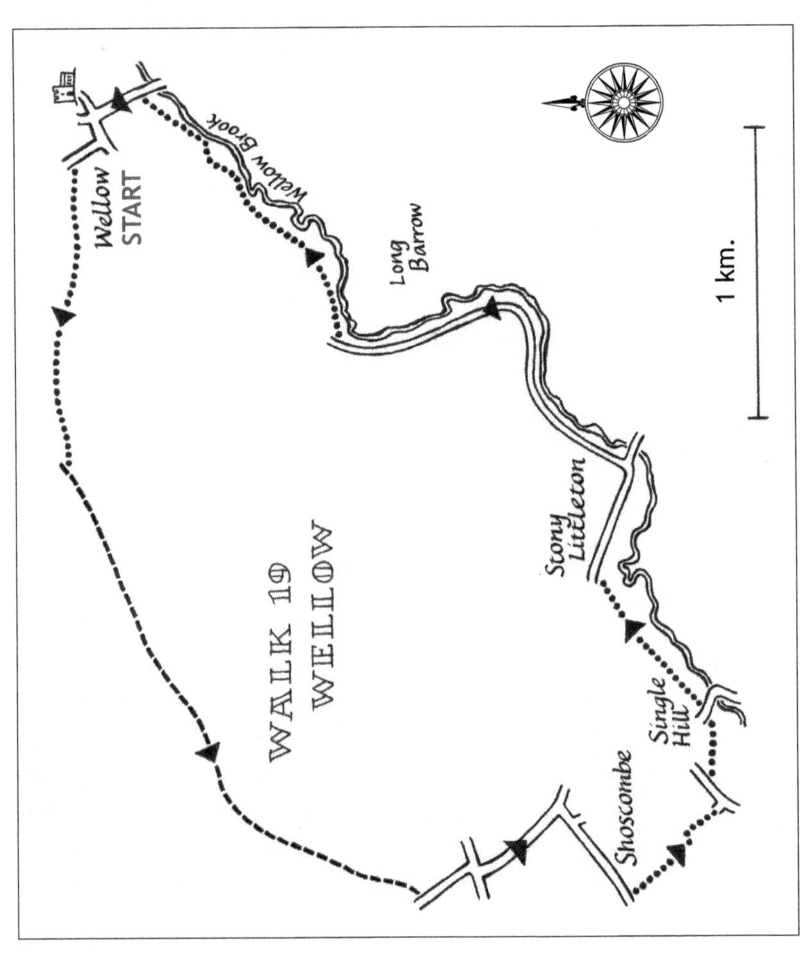

Wellow
START
Wellow Brook
Long Barrow
WALK 19
WELLOW
Stony Littleton
Single Hill
Shoscombe
1 km.

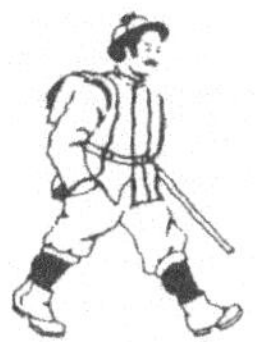

19 WELLOW

via Shoscombe and Single Hill

Distance:	9.5 km. 6 miles
Map:	Explorer 142
Map reference:	584742
Refreshments en route:	The Fox and Badger pub in Wellow;
	The Apple Tree Inn in Shoscombe

THE WALK follows ways between the two contrasting communities: Wellow is a sizable village with an ancient church, church school and pub; Shoscombe is a scattering of houses and cottages which mainly grew up around a colliery here – a shaft was dug in 1828 to a depth of 360 feet. It had ceased production before 1860 – and the later arrival of the Somerset and Dorset railway which served both locations before its closure in 1966. The walk from Wellow climbs up to a ridge offering fine views until a descent to Shoscombe, the half-way point. The pleasant return route to Wellow is by quiet lanes and riverside paths.

DIRECTIONS

Wellow church provides a good starting point for the walk, particularly as there is usually adequate space to park on the roadside here. With your back to the church, turn R. You will quickly reach the **Fox and Badger pub.**

Turn R up the road signposted to **Bath and Combe Hay**, passing **Weavers Orchard.** You will soon spot a PF sign indicating a route to your L. Locate the iron gates on your L, easily missed, and bear sharp L towards them where, tucked in at the R, is an iron gate. Cross here to a second gate and follow a leftward diagonal course which crosses the field towards a metal XG in the hedgerow opposite.

From this point continue to ascend by a lightly beaten path in the same diagonal direction to reach a Bristol gate near the top far corner.

> As you increase altitude you will enjoy increasingly wide views, first across the valley in which nestles Wellow. The tower of Wellow church is to the left and above it, on the skyline, the village of Hinton Charterhouse.

Continue the same course in this spacious field to reach a further field-to-field XG. Pass through another XG to reach a final one to exit the field path and access a grit track.

> From this vantage point you can look back and pick out Westbury White Horse on the rim of Salisbury Plain. The field you have just crossed is indicated on the OS map as ROMAN VILLA (site of), though there is no visible sign of this.

Bear L and follow this track for around a mile. You will pass an airstrip accompanied by a windsock on your L.

> On one occasion when I walked along here a small plane flew by trailing a banner which read 'Something Wonderful will Happen' (it didn't) and dropped it next to the strip (see picture opposite).

Some way along this track you reach a fork beside a barn: bear L here and continue by the main track. Eventually the path descends to meet a crossing of ways. Pass through the gate and walk on in the same direction. By now the din of traffic on the Wells road as it bypasses to the south of Peasedown St John becomes evident. Your track leads through a series of gates; the final one will drop you onto a lane where you turn left.

At the road junction cross over the slightly staggered junction (R and L) and carry on by the lane signposted to **Shoscombe**. Turn R at the first junction. There soon follows a steep descent towards the village.

The next stage of the walk is shown by a PF sign indicating a metalled footpath to the L – this is opposite a bus stop and sign indicating **Applecroft**. However, if you wish to visit the local pub you will find the **Apple Tree Inn** a little way further along the lane.

To continue the walk, head along the signed metalled path opposite Applecroft to reach the village school, housed in a Victorian building.

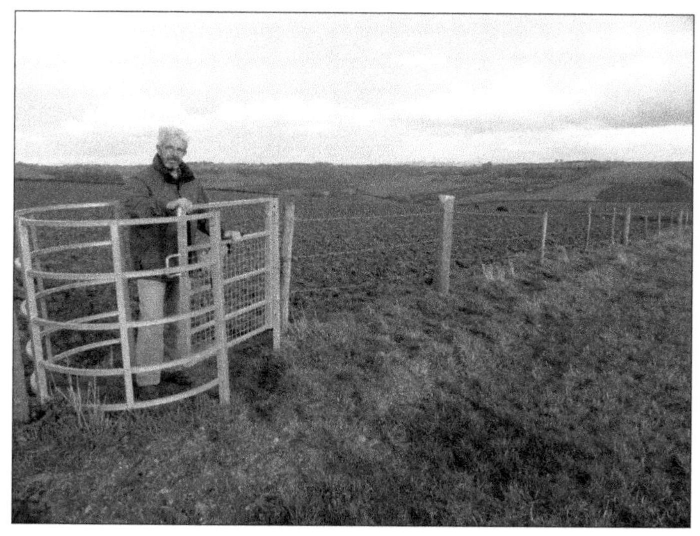

Final field-to-field kissing gate on the ascent from Wellow

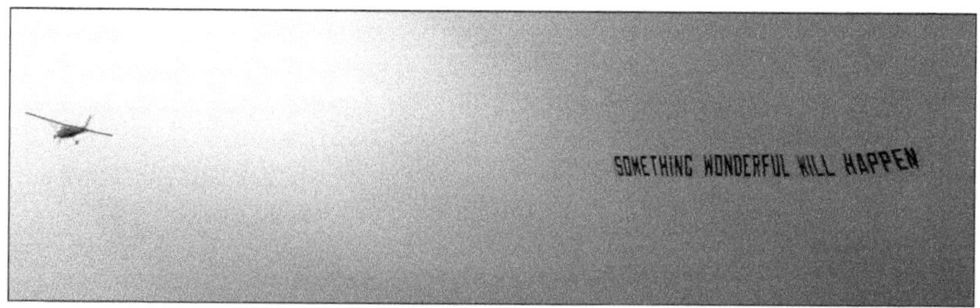

A hopeful message in the skies between Wellow and Shoscombe

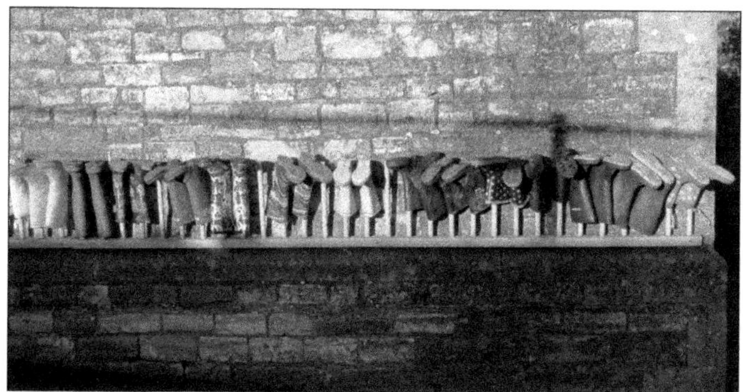

Children's wellies neatly parked outside Shoscombe primary school

Here turn L past the entrance to Shoscombe Church School. Now look out for a PF sign a hundred metres or so on your R, beside a row of houses called **Hamilton Terrace**. Follow the direction shown via a row of garages to reach the entrance to a field. Head diagonally to the L to exit at the bottom L corner. Carry on by the footpath until you reach a lane, then bear R and immediately L along a street of houses indicated as Single Hill.

> At the junction where you enter Single Hill, look out for an information board erected by Shoscombe History Group which details the former existence here of the Shoscombe and Single Hill Halt (1929–1966) on the Somerset and Dorset (S & D) Railway. There is even a quote from Arthur Conan Doyle who mentioned it in his writings.

Carry on past the houses and a former Chapel (Enlarged 1878), then by a narrow path which takes you to a field looking towards an arched railway bridge. Leave the field to reach a lane. Bear right across the former railway bridge and walk along the descending lane for 300 metres or so towards the Wellow Brook.

Turn L by a lane signposted as a **Byway** and **Sustrans** route indicating Wellow 1¾. This provides a pleasant and practically traffic-free stream-side walk for the next half-mile or so. You pass a Second World War pillbox and eventually reach a house opposite a bridge across Wellow Brook which will take you to **Stoney Littleton Long Barrow**.

Ignore this, unless you wish to visit the barrow (see Walk 19 in *Where Wiltshire Meets Somerset*), but continue to follow the brook for some distance. Keep alert for a metal XG on your right and an indicated PF. This way closely follows the brook all the way back to Wellow. You will spot the tower of St Julian's church en route.

You pass through three XGs and reach a final XG at a point where a footpath leads to L and R, with a row of cottages ahead. Past the cottages you emerge at a lane where you turn L to reach the crossroads at the centre of Wellow. *Or ......*

Alternatively, turn L at this junction of paths and climb past the former signal box of the S & D and on the the Fox and Badger pub. Turn R for the **church** and your starting point.

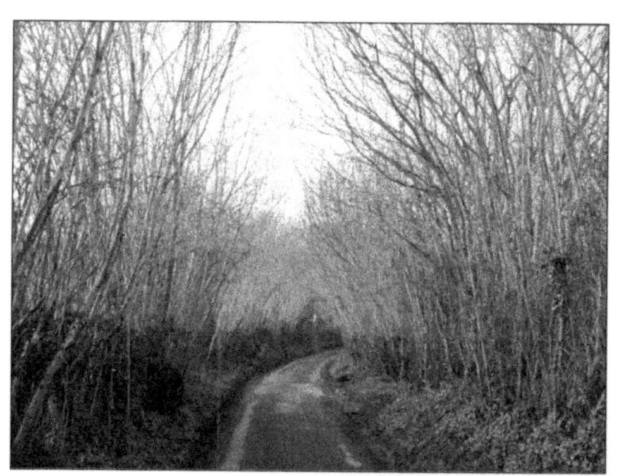

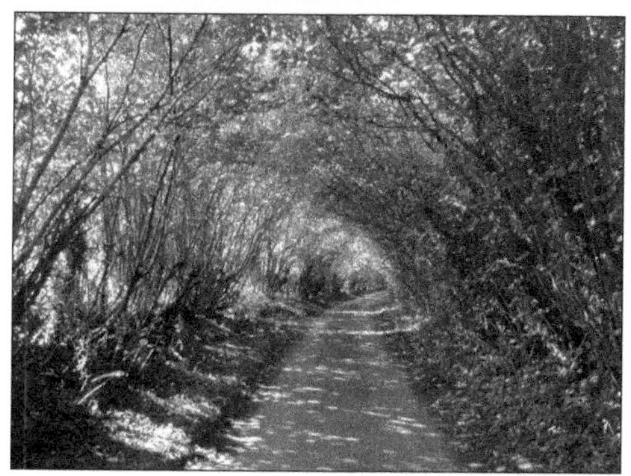

Above and right: The Sustrans route leading to Wellow, winter and summer

Below left: Fox and Badger pub, Wellow

Below right: St Julian's church tower, Wellow

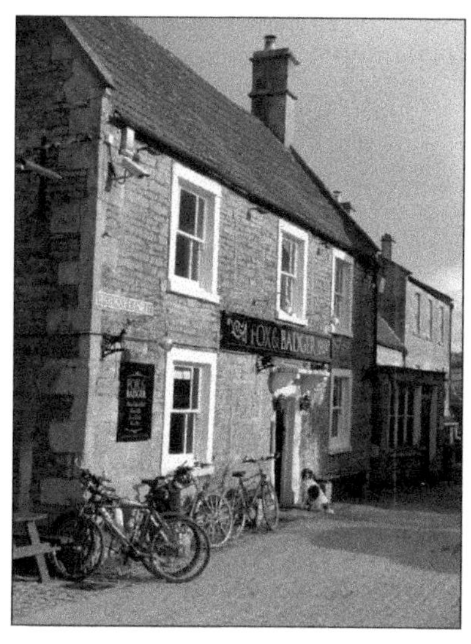

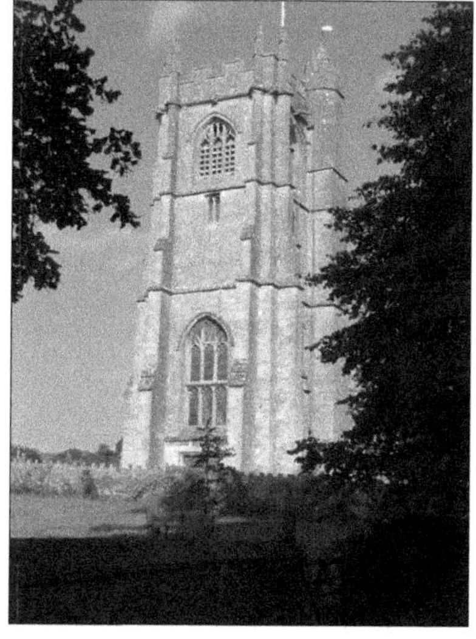

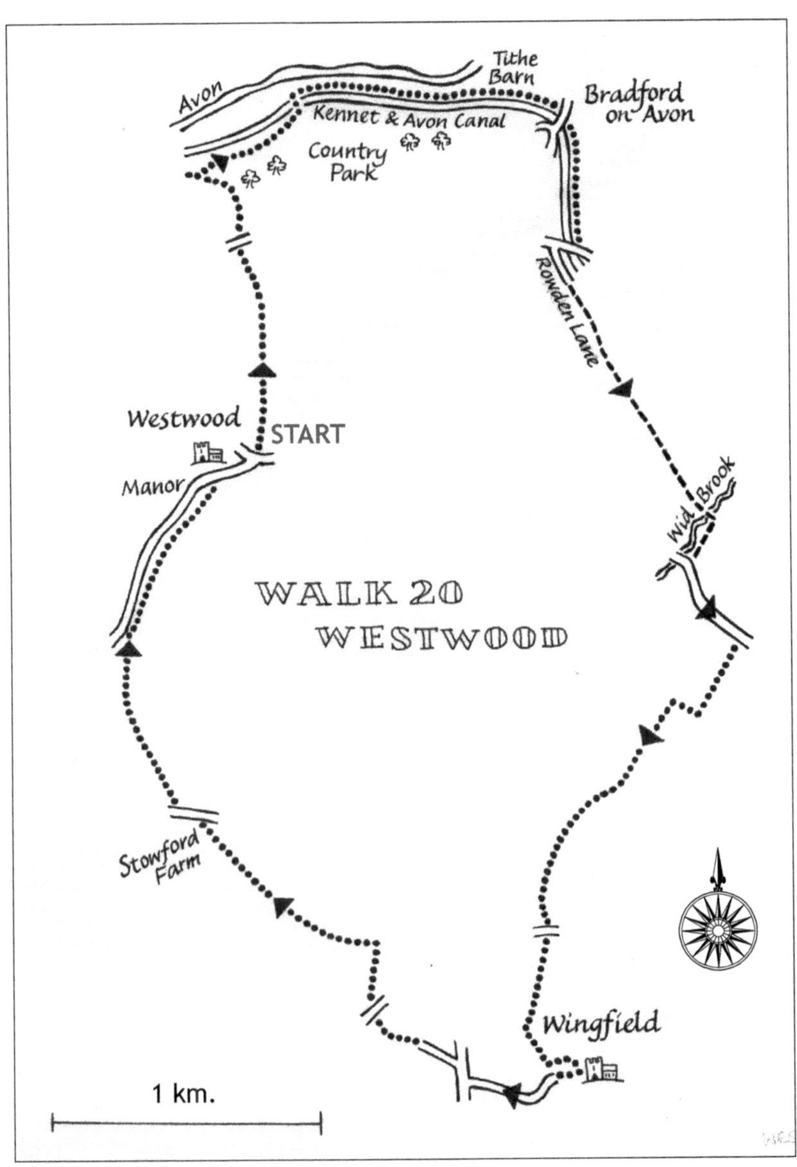

Avon
Tithe Barn
Bradford on Avon
Kennet & Avon Canal
Country Park
Rowden Lane
Westwood
START
Manor
Wid Brook
WALK 20
WESTWOOD
Stowford Farm
Wingfield
1 km.

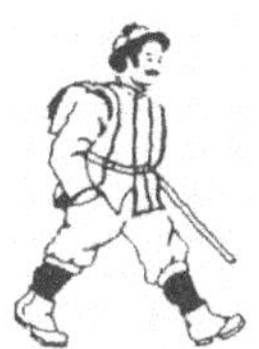

via Kennet & Avon Canal, Bradford on Avon, Wingfield and Stowford

Distance:	10¾ km. 6¾ miles
Map:	Explorers 143 and 156
Map reference:	590813
Refreshments en route:	Kennet & Avon Canal Trust Tea Shop and pubs where the canal approaches BoA; The Poplars pub at Wingfield, The New Inn at Westwood

THE WALK is a longish one and mostly on the level with the exception of a sharp descent to the Kennet & Avon Canal and a steady climb from Stowford towards Westwood. The starting point is the lovely group of buildings comprising the church and manor at Westwood, then across fields to reach the canal towpath towards Bradford on Avon's tithe barn and the bustle at Bradford Wharf. There are more field paths to complete the walk via Wingfield, Stowford and back to Westwood.

NOTE: *Unfortunately, a couple of stretches of road walking are unavoidable: from the end of Rowden Lane for around 400 metres and a very short stretch above at Stowford.*

DIRECTIONS

With your back to **Westwood church** and Manor bear L to the road junction and Upper Westwood's **New Inn.** Carry on past the pub entrance to cross a ST into a field. Walk directly ahead to reach a ST and field crossing. Once across bear slightly to the L to reach the next crossing, then a little to the L once again to a final ST which drops you onto the lane.

Note the directions given on the PF sign here: cross the lane and follow the direction shown opposite through the garden of number **102**. Once through the garden follow the path and cross a series of field crossings, keeping the hedgerow on your L.

At a third crossing descend directly downhill towards the canal below. Bear right and follow the canal-side path to reach the **footbridge** beside the swing bridge. Cross over to gain the **towpath** and bear R. As you approach the southern outskirts of Bradford on Avon you will pass the magnificent **tithe barn** on your L.

> Should you be in need of refreshment, there is a choice of watering holes. The Canal Tavern is on your L, opposite the Lock Inn. The K & A Trust Tea Room will be found a few yards along, opposite Bradford Wharf.

At the road bear R, cross over, and once again locate the **towpath** on your L. Continue past the beer garden of the Barge Inn opposite until you reach a **road bridge (number 171)** and climb the steps on your L.

Turn R and cross over, then turn L into **Rowden Lane**. You will pass **Sainsburys** on your R and various units which comprise the Treenwood Industrial Estate. Once past T & A Motors, Rowden Lane reverts to a rough track and later a green way flanked by hedges. You reach a wooden footbridge across the **Wid Brook**. Here you follow the track to the R to reach the road where you turn L.

There is now a stretch of unavoidable road walking in order to reach the next section of field path. Cross the road when there is a safe opportunity to do so. Look out for a PF sign opposite. Do not cross the ST here but carry on to reach a second PF sign beside a field gate – you will find this opposite a power installation on the L. Cross the ST here and head straight on following the hedgebank on your R. Follow the track beside the field edge which soon bears R past a stile, then L. Take the second opening on the R into an adjoining field and turn L to follow the tree line.

Carry on with the line of conifers on your L, past the track as it swerves L and beside the hedge to your L. Carry on to reach a wooden step ST and PF sign. Enter the field to your L and closely follow the field boundary to your L. Cross a second ST and finally a third beside a stone building. Now follow the drive past Trowle House with its eye-catching Dutch gables to reach the road.

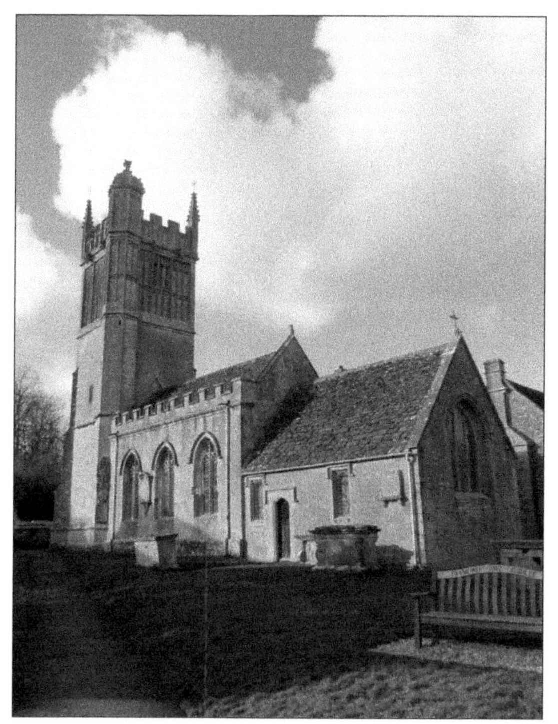

St Mary's church, Westwood

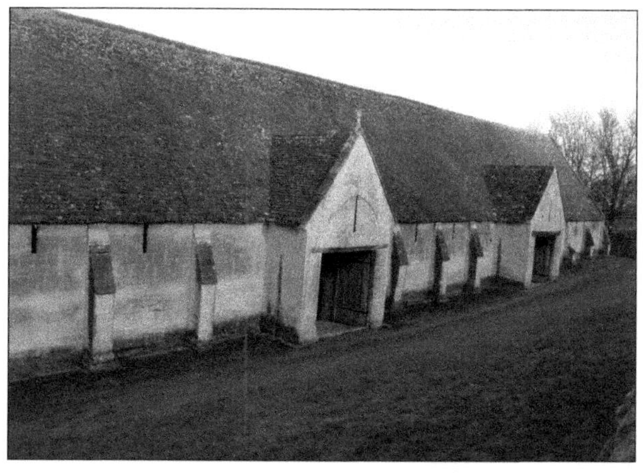

The Tithe Barn, Bradford-on-Avon, as seen from the Kennet & Avon Canal towpath, a huge and impressively proportioned 14th century structure

Cross over, with care, and continue by crossing the ST at the entrance to Church Farm, then follow the hedgerow on your L. The track becomes concreted where you will see across the field to your L to the tower of **Wingfield Church**. Carry on to the field corner to reach the double step ST and gate.

To visit the church, bear L to reach the lane and L via the gated path to the church. From the churchyard you will see red brick houses marking the outskirts of **Trowbridge**.

From the church, retrace your steps, head past the former Rectory and the village school, known as **The Mead Community Primary School.**

Note the memorial tablet in the entrance gable which records the founding of the school in 1849, 'a year of peculiar mercies'.

When you reach the main road you will see the Poplars pub opposite. Bear R, cross the road and then turn L along Shop Lane. As you pass the last dwelling here the way shrinks to a narrow path. Cross a couple of STs, then bear R across the field towards the barn where you will find a ST which drops you onto the lane. Now head for the ST a little to the R.

Once in this field head past the barn on your left to make for the exit by a ST just to the L of the **wooden fence** enclosing the house beyond. Cross here and follow the hedge on your R to reach a XG at a track. Bear R and immediately L by another XG. Now plot a course diagonally across the field to reach a ST in the fence opposite, about 100 metres to the left of a solitary oak tree. Continue in the same direction towards a ST in the far L corner. There is another stile opposite, then a final one which drops you onto the road where you bear L.

This road is often busy and there is neither pavement nor grass verge. Thankfully we only need negotiate the road for a few metres towards **Stowford Farm** where we cross over to reach the junction of a pair of tracks. There is a map posted here which shows local footpaths.

Take the stony track to the L which climbs the hillside and eventually levels out. You reach a ST on the R to enter a field where you follow the beaten path to an exit in the far L corner. In doing so you cross a wide groove near the centre - this is a trace of the main street which served the lost medieval village of Rowley (see photo opposite).

When you reach the lane look out for a ST immediately on the R - this will lead you along a path which follows a hedgebank before regaining the lane near **Westwood Church** and your starting point.

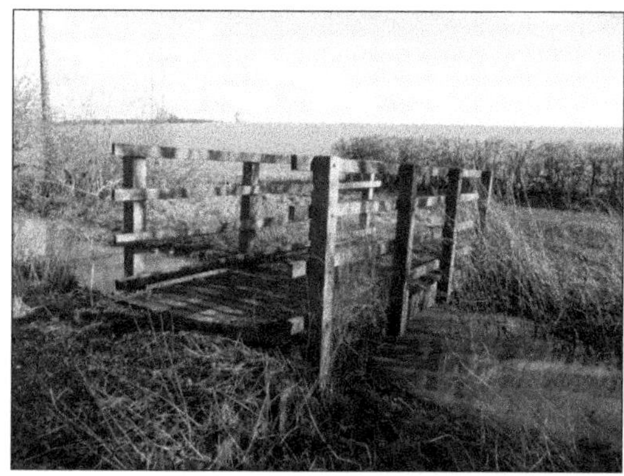

Footbridge crossing
Wid Brook
Rowden Lane

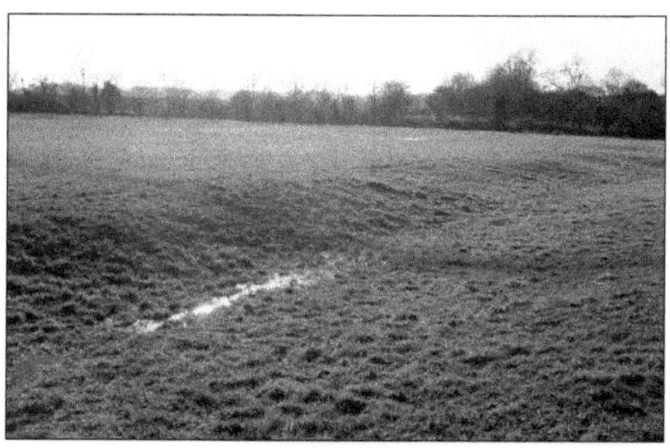

Trace of main street through the deserted village of Rowley. For a thorough account see *A History of Rowley-Wittenham: Deserted Medieval Village and Lost Parish* (BoA Museum, 2022)

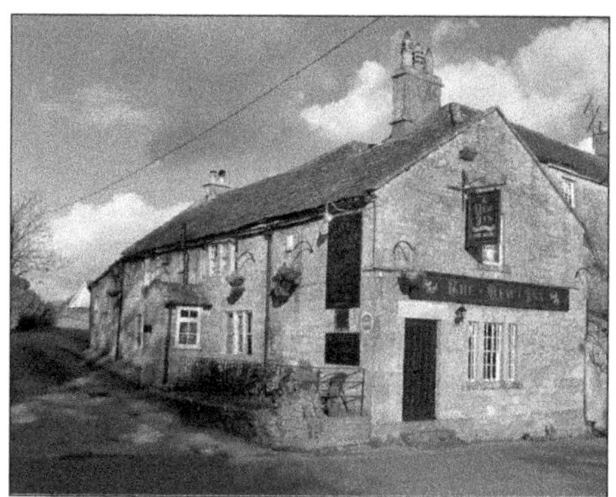

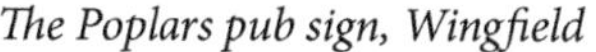

The Poplars pub sign, Wingfield

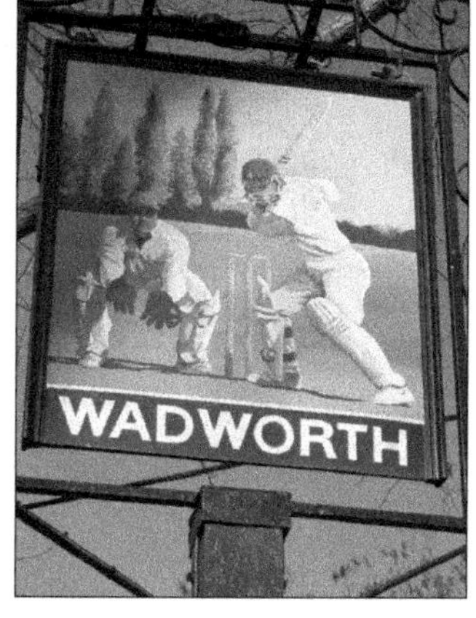

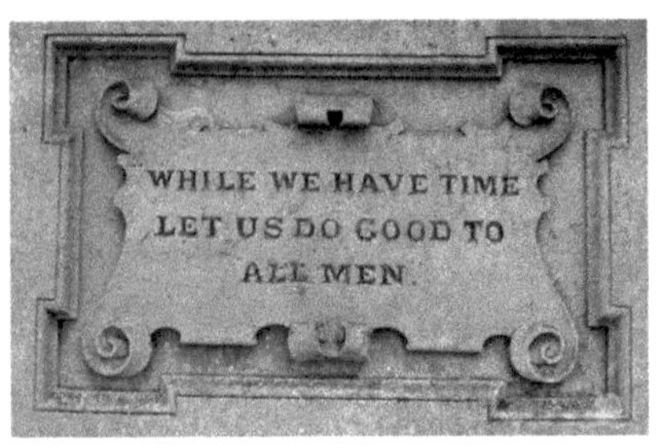

… and women!

Inscription on monument at Colerne

Also published by Ex Libris Press ~

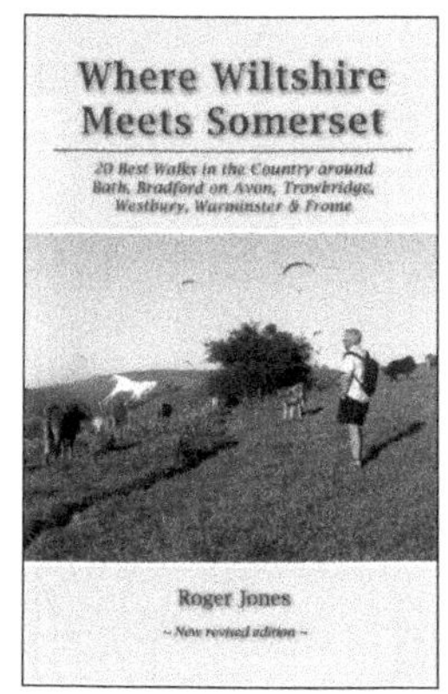

WHERE WILTSHIRE MEETS SOMERSET
20 best walks in the country around Bath, Bradford on Avon, Trowbridge, Westbury, Warminster & Frome

by Roger Jones

128 pages; Illustrated with drawings & sketch maps
ISBN 1-906641-55-9
Newly revised edition 2019; Price £7.95

This book is the precursor of and uniform with the present volume.

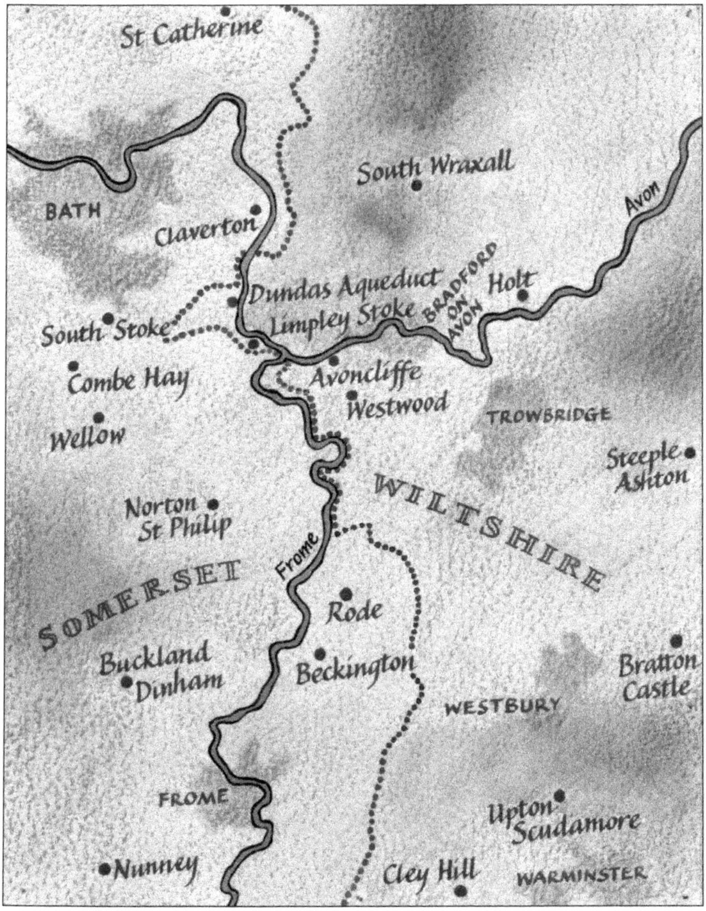

Map showing the starting points of the walks featured in Where Wiltshire Meets Somerset